My Boys and Girls Are in There

My Boys and Girls Are in There

The 1937 New London School Explosion

Ron Rozelle

Texas A&M University Press   *College Station*

LIBRARY OF CONGRESS CATALOGING-IN-PUBLICATION DATA

Rozelle, Ron, 1952–
    My boys and girls are in there : the 1937 New London school explosion / Ron Rozelle.
        p.   cm.
    Includes bibliographical references and index.
    ISBN-13: 978-1-60344-761-4 (cloth : alk. paper)
    ISBN-10: 1-60344-761-X (cloth : alk. paper)
    ISBN-13: 978-1-60344-780-5 (e-book)
    ISBN-10: 1-60344-780-6 (e-book)
    1. Consolidated School (New London, Tex.)—Explosion, 1937. 2. School accidents—Texas—New
London—History—20th century. 3. Explosions—Texas—New London—History—20th century.
4. Natural gas—Accidents—Texas—New London—History—20th century. 5. New London
(Tex.)—History—20th century. 6. Disaster victims—Texas—New London—Biography. 7. New
London (Tex.)—Biography. I. Title.
LD7501.N4662R69 2012
372.9764'185—dc23
                                                                                                2011037290

To New Londoners,
past and present.

A voice was heard in Ramah,
Weeping and great mourning,
Rachel weeping for her children;
And she refused to be comforted,
Because they were no more.

—Matthew 2:18

The Greeks said that no one is ever dead, truly dead,
until no one remembers them
and no one speaks their name.

—John Fuhr, a survivor,
at the 1977 anniversary of the
London Consolidated School disaster

Contents

A Note

Since artistic license—though subtle, and very little of it—has been employed to make *My Boys and Girls Are in There* read like a story and not a report, it might be well to quote the legendary Texas author John Graves at the outset. Before spinning his fine *Goodbye to a River* he informed the reader that though it was not a work of fiction, it had some fictionalizing in it. "Its facts are factual," he wrote, "and the things it says happened did happen."

Such is the case here.

In telling the story of the New London disaster, no characters were created that did not actually exist, nor were any names changed. In a few cases, characters whose families could not be located for interviews were provided personalities that will hopefully bring them, and the story as a whole, more fully alive.

Those parts of the narrative that relate specific times, statistics, and important events or decisions are the results of considerable digging though archives, old newspapers, transcripts of survivor's recollections, and official documents.

But descriptions of the daily goings-on in a small East Texas town were sometimes conjured by an author who grew up in one, and paid attention.

Prologue

T he woods are thick there. Stately oaks and sycamores are plentiful, and cedars, and a great abundance of pines that rise up specter-like through lesser trees. The woods in that place are lovely, dark, and deep, like Robert Frost's New England woods of a century ago.

But they constantly give over completely and unexpectedly to vast open pastures of rippling grass that slope gracefully against the dark curtains of more trees on their distant edges.

In the town, a few buildings and houses hug close to the highway, like things that have collected at a drain after a deluge. Other houses sit further back and up in the hills, and some in the long valleys. There is a convenience store that sells gas, microwaved pizzas, and sandwiches, lotto tickets, and just enough groceries to fend off driving three miles to the Brookshire Brothers' supermarket in the next town. There is a small branch office of a bank, a do-nut shop, and not much else in the way of commerce.

There are two churches, Baptist and Methodist, and there is the handsome school that fronts the highway that some very old people still call the new school, even though it was built long, long ago.

On a small island in the middle of State Highway 42 there is a pink granite cenotaph soaring up, complete with classical figures carved into the apex. It's the sort of imposing monument one would expect to see in a city rather than in the middle of a tiny town, much less in the middle of a highway. It is flanked on one side by the school and, on the other, by a combination café, soda fountain, tea shop, and museum.

The school, the monument, and the museum are, of course, the things that set the town completely apart from any number of similar hamlets sprinkled throughout the piney woods of eastern Texas.

If there are ghosts there, in the town or the school or the woods, they are quiet about it. And decidedly not malicious.

People have maintained, for three quarters of a century, that there must surely be ghosts. But most would concur that they wouldn't be of the lost soul variety. For most of them died within a short walk of where they had been born, and in the brief interval between their birth and their death few had ventured very far. So, if they are there, they are most certainly not lost. They're home.

Many of their graves are in a cemetery several miles east of town, but others are in burying grounds out in the country, and some are in towns far and near. Now, after so long a time, their parents and grandparents have joined them, people who stood at open bedroom doors looking at perfectly made beds, at baseballs that would never be thrown kept on tops of polished dressers, at hair ribbons that would never be worn hanging from mirrors. At any number of things preserved for a time like parts of shrines before being packed carefully away in attics and trunks.

Finally enough time passed for the parents and grandparents to hand over the remembering and grieving and the constant groping for some remotely viable reason, or an explanation, or for something intangible as smoke that became fashionable to call closure. All of this was left, finally, to siblings and to friends. To survivors.

It's hard going, a difficult business indeed, being a survivor.

In that place—in the woods and fields and the town—there is a cacophony of sounds at the very ends of days. The pumps of a few remaining oil wells, their steel derricks long since removed, still provide a soft, pulsating melody that floats along almost unnoticed, as natural as birdsong and wind.

In the gloaming, when daylight yields slowly to darkness, birds communicate in high-pitched warbles, crickets and cicadas chirp, and country dogs—free rangers unfenced and unchained—bark way up in the hills. Sometimes one sends up a somber, sorrowful howl, and occasionally a hawk will screech out a note or two and float gracefully over everything.

In the very last moments of the transition, when daylight is straining to stay, the sounds of creatures usually die completely away and leave the place to the sweep and whoosh of soft wind in the tops of the tall trees.

Some will tell you the wind sounds, on those late afternoons, like a mixture of laughter and chattering and contentedness.

Some will tell you it sounds like the voices of children.

Part One

"My Boys and Girls"

One

The night had been just chilly enough to require a light quilt over the bedspread. An hour before daylight Floy Dees rubbed her hands together for a satisfying moment over the gas flame on the stove before she slid her heavy iron skillet onto the grate.

Soon the fragrance of sizzling bacon brought Marvin in yawning, buttoning his shirt. He poured himself a cup of coffee, drifted his hand across the back of Floy's neck, and watched the three rig flares that he could see from the kitchen window.

They liked to sit on the front porch at night and watch the bluish white flames, and sometimes they got in the car and drove up to a hilltop that offered a wide panorama of thousands of flickering lights. Floy had told him one night that it was almost like the oil companies had lit them all to give everybody something pretty to enjoy, like more candles than you could count underneath a sky full of even more stars. Marvin had laughed at that, and told her the companies didn't care one bit about pretty things, but only about making money. Natural gas that came up with oil was a worthless commodity, and what wasn't needed to fire the boilers that powered each rig's pump and other machinery had to be flared off.

She knew that, of course. But she liked the notion of candles better.

When they sat down and ate their breakfast the scraping of silverware against plates was the only sound other than the soft, sliding rhythm of the trio of pumps located close by. They both were twenty-one, and had only been married for a little over two years, but they didn't feel the need to chatter away through a conversation when one wasn't needed, being that confident of each other that they could sit quietly through a meal or a radio show or a drive.

They had grown up together, in nearby Troup. When they'd finished the eleventh grade, which was as high as grades went in county schools, they married, which was as logical and natural a step as Marvin's gravitation to the oil field.

There was a quick kiss at the door after he put on his jacket and made sure he had his work gloves in the pockets. Then she handed him his metal lunch box with a small thermos of coffee inside the rounded top and watched as he started off up the dark road to the local headquarters of the Texas Company, one of a legion of oil concerns that had set up field offices seven years before.

Marvin's walk was shorter than most workers', only two hundred yards or thereabouts. Floy watched him from the porch until she couldn't see him anymore. She knew that in a few minutes he'd step out of the darkness into the bright light of busy industry, where big floodlights illuminated parked trucks, a yard stacked with piles of various lengths of steel pipe, a warehouse, and a small office that didn't look any more grandiose than the other structures made of wood and corrugated tin. Once there he'd fall in with his crew and they'd gas up their truck, fill a big cooler with ice and water, and wait until their foreman got his orders from the field superintendent. Then they'd head off to a lease and do whatever needed doing until quitting time.

Floy shivered just a bit as the first pink vein of pale sunlight showed itself over the top of a thick stand of pines and cedars. She decided that later, when the sun had been up long enough to burn off the morning chill, she'd drive over to her uncle's store in Henry's Chapel and buy some groceries.

She looked one last time, before turning to go inside, at the road that Marvin had just walked up. Then she caught herself smiling as she thought of him finding his favorite supper that afternoon when he came back down it.

≈

Seven miles away, in New London, Virgie Abercrombie looked out at the early morning sky through the window over her kitchen sink and listened to her boys finishing their breakfasts. She would have hers later, after Boyd and Dalton had left for school and Talmage, her youngest, was either down for a nap or sprawled out on the floor with one of the new pups.

Virgie normally wouldn't have even considered letting an animal in her house, but she'd recently relented. Talmage was recovering from extensive surgery to correct his defective legs, which were now encased in a pair of heavy plaster casts. Since he couldn't do the roaming around that two-year-olds naturally do, she brought the pup in occasionally to keep him entertained.

She glanced at the clock on her kitchen wall and told the boys to hurry up or they'd be late. She'd cooked the first breakfast for her husband Eric long before daylight, even before he rolled slowly out of their bed and pulled on coarse khaki pants, two shirts, and great clunky boots for another long day in the oil fields. Later she'd prepared another batch of scrambled eggs, fried ham, and buttermilk biscuits for the boys. In a little while, when everyone was gone except for Talmage and herself, she would make do with whatever was left over. If nothing was, she'd treat herself to a slice of pound cake and a last cup of coffee.

Boyd, the oldest, mopped up the last of his eggs with what was left of a thick biscuit and sloshed it down with frothy milk. When he dragged his shirtsleeve across his mouth he winked across the table at Talmage and broke into a few twangy lines from a song he'd heard the Light Crust Doughboys sing on the radio the night before.

Dalton and his mother watched until Boyd was finished then they looked at each other, both of them at a loss as to where all his bluster came from. His parents were quiet people, and Dalton was so shy that he might go an entire day without saying a single word to anyone other than a teacher who asked him a direct question.

But a generous dollop of blarney had tumbled down from somewhere and lodged in Boyd, who, at sixteen, was already adept at talking pure nonsense to anyone who would listen, especially pretty girls. The Abercrombies were new to town, along with many other families who'd come so their men could work in the oil field as long as possible before going home again. But Boyd had settled in as if he'd been raised there. In other parts of the nation he might have been compared to a young Lincoln; he was that gangly, with huge hands and feet, and he had that many stories to tell. But in eastern Texas not enough old people that still held Lincoln personally responsible for a multitude of sins had died by 1937 to let such a similarity count as a compliment.

Talmage hooted and clapped in his highchair when Boyd finished the song, which earned him another wink.

The rest of the little family—little, at least, by rural standards of that era, when households often ran to nine or more children—could no more account for the special bond between Boyd and Talmage than they could for Boyd's jocund personality. The oldest brother had laid claim to the youngest since shortly after his birth. When Virgie would go to bathe Talmage, feed him, or put him to bed she often as not discovered that Boyd had already done it.

Virgie looked at the clock again, slapped her dish towel against her thigh, and said she meant it about them being late. Dalton grabbed up books and tablets and scooted out, letting the screen door slap twice against the door frame. Boyd went over and gave his mother a quick peck on her cheek that made her grin and slap his back with her towel. Then he leaned down and kissed the top of Talmage's head.

Finally, for some reason that Virgie would never be able to explain in the seven decades that would be left to her, Boyd rubbed his hand gently along one of Talmage's thick casts and told his mother to never whip those legs.

Two

What people called New London was not really a town at all, at least not officially. The residents of the small settlement of London had to go to nearby Overton, which was really no great burden since it was all of three miles away, to mail a letter or receive one, so somebody filled out the necessary paperwork to apply for a post office. In due course the government denied the request because a London, Texas, already existed, west of Austin in Kimble County, near Junction. So the apparently illegitimate Londoners simply marched several hundred yards due north, near where the new consolidated school had been built in 1932, and christened the place New London. By 1937 everybody used the new name, but the post office wouldn't be built until a year later.

That there was a London at all, new or old, was because the men who farmed and worked in sawmills needed somewhere to live and raise their families.

It was born because of timber and farming, but its new prosperity was owing to oil.

The East Texas field had been discovered in 1930 when a wildcatter named Columbus Marion "Dad" Joiner drilled the Daisy Bradford #3, the first two wells of that name having proven to be dusters. The third time was most definitely the charm and by 1937 so many wells were dug that woodlands and pastures and towns were covered with thousands of derricks, each housing a pulsating pump that ran continuously.

In Kilgore, the town with the good fortune to be located directly above the richest lode, the derricks were so thick downtown that they became hazards to navigation. Roads that had been in place for decades had to be rerouted; stores had to be pulled down and built in other places. The faithful attended Sunday morning services and Wednesday night prayer meetings in churches surrounded by derricks, and sang hymns as the pumps thumped along like so many giant metronomes.

New London, nine miles southwest of Kilgore, didn't have as many derricks as its larger neighbor. But it had plenty.

Anyone having heard the town's name and expecting to find a quaint New England village filled with steep-roofed cottages, ivy covered chimneys, and an abundance of narrow steeples pointing heavenward would have been disappointed. The wood frame houses and stores that made up the place were almost universally utilitarian, having been constructed because of the lumber trade. Then, when the oil fields came in, the economy had taken a giant leap forward—ironically, less than a year after the stock market crash—but the architecture and ambiance had stayed put. Big oil corporations came in and slapped together company houses quickly, each plain structure a cookie cutter duplicate of those on either side of it.

In other parts of the world, Franklin Delano Roosevelt had just been sworn in for a second term and his New Deal was having difficulty finding its feet, the Spanish Civil War was raging, and Hitler was rubbing his small hands together, ready to gobble up Europe. The *Hindenburg* was making regular trans-Atlantic crossings, and Shirley Temple was the top box office draw.

None of this meant very much to the residents of Rusk County, except perhaps the bit about Shirley Temple. Most folks occasionally drove into Henderson or Kilgore or Tyler to see a picture show.

One family had recently made the long trek over to Dallas and came back telling of a new contraption called an automat, where you could plug a coin into a slot, open a little glass door, and lift out a ham sandwich or a wedge of pie. The women found it interesting. But most of the men figured having somebody sit hot food in front of them on a table was preferable.

At half past seven on the morning of Thursday, March 18, most of the men of New London were at work in the oil fields; their wives were going about their morning chores.

And their children were making their way to school.

Three

In Tyler, the largest of East Texas's towns and twenty-five miles west of New London, Mother Mary Ambrose Krueger, the resident superior of the Sisters of the Holy Family of Nazareth, was going over the particulars of what would be a very long day.

The order's brand new facility would be dedicated the next afternoon, March 19, the Feast Day of Saint Joseph, and blessed by Bishop Joseph Patrick Lynch of Dallas. Then the keys to Mother Francis Hospital would be ceremoniously handed over to Mother Mary Ambrose by the state director of the Works Progress Administration—FDR's famous WPA, which built the imposing edifice—and its doors would open to the public for the first time.

It was a handsome, white four-story building on a hilltop, modeled after the Duke University hospital in Durham, North Carolina, with sixty beds, modern surgical and treatment facilities, and an ornate chapel. It would be the largest hospital between Dallas and New Orleans, and would provide medical attention to a geographical area the size of several northeastern states combined.

But all of that would start after the big doings planned for the next day. The bishop would preside, assisted by the pastor of Tyler's Immaculate Conception parish, over the dedication and consecration, which would be attended by local civic leaders and a couple of legislators coming up by train from Austin. Mother Mary Regina, the Provincial Superior, was due to arrive in the early afternoon and, shortly after that, a florist would deliver big arrangements of fresh-cut flowers for the lobby and the chapel.

There was already a stack of congratulatory telegrams on Mother Mary Ambrose's desk from communities of nuns from her order throughout the nation, along with a couple from Rome. One was from Mother Mary Lauretta Lubowidzka, the Superior General of the order, and another conveyed the paternal and apostolic benediction of Pope Pius the Eleventh, signed by his

Secretary of State Cardinal Eugenio Pacelli, who in two years' time would become Pope Pius the Twelfth.

On this early morning the superintendent of the new hospital and her staff had a good many things to see to. And Mother Mary Ambrose, who could be something of a taskmaster when it was called for, figured today it was called for.

So she went over her list once more with the sixteen nodding nuns and ten graduate nurses who had already heard the recitation several times in the last few days.

Four

W. C. Shaw, the superintendent of the London Consolidated School District, stood at his office window and watched the Abercrombie boys cross the wide front lawn with other children who walked from their homes in town. Those who lived out in the country filed out of a line of yellow buses parked on the narrow road that ran between the junior high and high school building and the elementary school.

Mr. Shaw was a beanpole of a man, always dapper in a three-piece suit and perfectly knotted tie. He wore a handsome fedora all the time when he was outside, and never indoors, which was the commonly observed rule in a time when most men wore hats. Thick wire-rimmed spectacles added to his overall stoic visage.

He watched the younger Abercrombie boy follow along after his big brother like a rowboat in the wake of a sleeker, speedier craft. Boyd, the older one, was already talking to whoever he had fallen in beside. He might even, Mr. Shaw thought as he squinted to see better, be singing.

The superintendent allowed himself a moment of quiet contemplation before the first bell sounded. It would be a busy day. Tomorrow there would be no school because many of his students would be competing in athletic and academic events at the county meet held every spring in Henderson, the county seat. Today teachers and coaches would be utilizing every moment they could find to make sure their charges were ready.

The Parent-Teacher Association would meet in the gymnasium in the afternoon, which meant Mr. Shaw was expected to go over there before the meeting and drink some punch, eat a cookie, watch some sort of dance or skit put on by an elementary class, and then say a few words and answer a multitude of questions.

He looked at the blue horizon over the dark woods in the hills, then his eyes searched beyond the buildings and rooftops of the town for the first white blossoms of dogwoods. Out there, not much more than a stone's throw from his school, was primeval forest—as yet uncleared except by oil companies to drill new wells—that covered sleeping hills and steep bluffs over creeks. The pine needle-covered ground in the densest parts was dark as night all the time, full of white-tailed deer and occasional wild hogs. In what seemed like eons ago he had bounded through those woods with other boys his age, chasing yapping dogs after raccoons. Now his youngest son, Sam, who had come in just a few minutes before to get his lunch money before rushing off to class, did too.

Mr. Shaw had been the superintendent at nearby Minden before the oil field was discovered, when timber had been the only industry, and schools had muddled along on pitifully small budgets. Then the deep wells were dug and the big companies had steadily pulled prime grade crude up from prehistoric reservoirs, which meant Rusk County had benefited greatly. Even in the midst of the current depression, which had not yet been paired with the adjective "great."

The influx of oilfield workers and their families, most of them having come from other places, had meant a new school would be needed to accommodate a student population many times larger than had attended the small, old, two-story schoolhouse in Overton. So the London Consolidated District had been created in 1932 and Mr. Shaw was appointed superintendent.

The building in which he now stood, housing grades five through eleven, barely four years old and over two hundred and fifty feet long, was a shining example of the area's good fortune. No costs had been spared (to the final tune of over three hundred thousand dollars for this building alone) in the construction of the steel-framed brick and masonry E-shaped structure, which housed state-of-the-art classrooms, science labs, vocational and homemaking facilities, and a library unrivaled in any public school. Instead of a noisy, cantankerous boiler, seventy-two shiny gas heaters filled the rooms, each attached to a pipe suspended on hangers that wound its way around a cavernous crawlspace beneath the eight-inch concrete floor, which rested on square foot cement piers. On Friday nights in autumn the Wildcats played football in the first high-school stadium in Texas to be illuminated by electric lights.

Because of the sudden influx of funds from several oil wells on school property and the recently expanded tax base, not a single bond had had to be voted on or sold to build the junior high and high school building, the elementary school, a big gymnasium, the stadium, and several outbuildings. The total cost of the project had been one million dollars.

But Mr. Shaw knew that even a great financial boom was no excuse to be anything less than a careful steward of the district's resources. He hadn't thought twice about asking the school board, just two months ago, to cancel their contract with the United Gas Company and allow him to have his janitors tap into the bleed off lines from the oil field. After all, most everybody he knew used the free gas in their homes, including most or all of the members of the board. Thrift, thrift, he often preached to his faculty, even in using chalk down to the nubbins before getting out new sticks. And what sort of leader would he be if he didn't practice what he preached?

From his window he looked out at the last arrivals as they made their way into his school. He tucked his thumbs in his vest pockets; the bright sunshine of a fine March morning reflected off the perfectly polished lenses of his spectacles. The American and Texas flags shifted leisurely in a soft breeze on the tall, gleaming pole beside the front sidewalk.

A few minutes earlier, as Mr. Shaw had stepped into classrooms to say good morning to some of his faculty, he'd found an English teacher writing on the slate blackboard at the front of her room. It read, in her precise cursive that dipped and rose like small waves on a lake:

Oil and natural gas are East Texas' greatest natural blessings. Without them this school would not be here and none of us would be here learning our lessons.

Five

A rdyth Davidson was running late.

She bolted down a piece of toast slathered with mayhaw jelly her mother had made her bring in the car. She had wanted neither the toast nor the plaid coat she was holding in her lap, upon which a smidgen of the amber jelly had already dropped.

She'd have to change into her softball uniform during lunch period, and the coat would be a burden to keep up with all day. But her mother had been adamant; the first day of spring was still a few days away, and mornings and evenings had been chilly. Ardyth was the only child of parents who had no plans to have another. So, unlike many of her friends that had houses full of siblings, she was a tad overprotected. Since she wouldn't be getting home from her game in Henderson until after dark, the coat was going. Period.

She'd taken longer with her hair this morning. A photographer was scheduled to take a picture of the softball team after lunch and she, at fourteen and fairly new to paying attention to hairdos and makeup and the boys who might take notice of such things, wanted to look good for it. The bulky uniform wasn't the classiest attire to be photographed in, she realized, but she had no control over that.

What she did have some control over was getting to school on time.

So she told her mother to drive faster.

≈

Three miles out the highway to Henderson twelve-year-old Doris Shoemate and her mother had started the morning with a little spat over something so trivial that whatever caused it would be lost forever.

But it had been enough of a disagreement for Doris to opt to walk down to the bus stop at the highway rather than be driven there, with her younger sister and brother, by their mother.

When they'd passed her on the road she hadn't looked in the direction of the car. Then, a few minutes later when Sammie and Elbert had been dropped off their mother had waved at her on the return trip.

But Doris had kept her gaze locked directly ahead of her and hugged her books tightly to her chest.

At the bus stop she said good morning to a couple of other children and then stood quietly beside her brother and sister, who were used to such goings on by now and just looked down the highway for the bus.

≈

In New London the owner and proprietor of Hartfield's Store, not far up the highway from the school, stood on the walkway in front of his establishment and admired the pyramid of cans of sliced peaches he had erected in the front window.

The fabric awning above him rustled slowly as he looked for any imperfection in the display. The week before he'd painted the specials on the window with a thick paste of Bon Ami cleaning powder and water. Then, when the specials were over, he'd gone at the glass with nothing more than a pail of water and a scrub brush, the liberal application of the Bon Ami making it fairly sparkle in bright sunlight.

He said good morning to one of his regular customers and held the door open for her as she went in for things she'd need for her family's supper. Or for a length of fabric cut to measure from a bolt. Or for a bottle of Baby Percy's Tonic if someone in the family was sickly, or an icy cold soda pop pulled from a deep reach-in cooler. Perhaps she needed a sack of the popular flour that the Light Crust Doughboys sang about on their radio program or a slab of souse (hog's head cheese) sliced out of a heavy crock kept on top of the meat counter beside a round of bright yellow, oily cheddar which was never refrigerated and everybody called "rat cheese."

When the lady went in Mr. Hartfield looked again at his handiwork and wiped a miniscule smudge away with the bottom of his apron.

There, in the glistening window, stood a perfect reflection of himself, of a cloudless sky as blue as a deep lake, and of the attractive front of the new school building just down the road.

Six

By midmorning the breeze died down to nothing and an agreeable day settled into place.

Virgie Abercrombie finished the wash and was hanging it out to dry on the line Eric had stretched from the shed to the back of the house. Talmage sat on the back porch petting the puppy, which had gone to sleep and snored loud enough for Virgie to hear it from the yard.

She planned out the rest of her day while she took one wooden clothes pin after another from the deep pocket of her apron and pinched them to the drawers and shirts and socks that hung wet and bleach-pungent in the sun. She'd dust the furniture later and give the kitchen floor a good scrubbing. In the early afternoon she would read Talmage a page or two from the storybook that she'd read to his brothers when they'd been little. Hopefully, he'd nod off and she could have a little quiet time in which to do her ironing before the older boys got home.

She'd been intending to make teacakes for several days and she resolved to do it today, to have them ready with mugs of hot chocolate when the boys arrived. She always used her mother's recipe and her cookies, big as flapjacks, were every bit as good—sweet and buttery and crinkle hard at the edges—as the ones she'd eaten as a little girl.

She missed her mother, and wished they could go back to Louisiana more often to see her. She hadn't made any close friends in New London, since many of the people here had grown up together, and others, like herself, were only here until the oil boom played itself out. People were nice enough, she figured, and especially so at church, but Virgie understood the difference in knowing someone for a year or so and knowing others as long as you've known anything. They had moved so Eric could find work in the oil field, which he'd had no difficulty doing. Since the East Texas field came in the unemployment crisis that crippled most of the nation was nowhere to be found in places sitting over oil. Able men who didn't mind doing hard work on the rigs from sunup to sundown could have steady jobs.

The Abercrombies could get by on Eric's salary, but the medical expenses for Talmage's surgery had been high. The clerks at the hospital in Dallas had told them that there was talk of some sort of financial relief on the way from the government, but it hadn't broken loose yet. It would be another year before the March of Dimes would come into being. So she and Eric were doing what most people did: paying the hospital and the doctor what they could when they could.

At least her baby's legs would be better now. She was too afraid to hope that they'd ever be perfect.

She prayed when she remembered to do it. For Talmage mostly, for his legs. And for the older boys; that Dalton would find some sort of confidence and that Boyd might tone his down a bit.

She prayed for more money, which must have blended in conveniently with many million versions of the same prayer every day of the 1930s. And she tried hard to count her blessings, like the preacher said to do on Sunday mornings. One blessing was an abundant spring garden and plenty of rainfall so far to sustain it. Another was free natural gas for the house, since Eric had tapped into the bleed off lines from the fields, a procedure as uncomplicated—at least for a roughneck—as slipping a pair of short c-shaped metal collars over the exposed line, bolting them tightly together, drilling a hole through a small protruding conduit, and attaching a long enough pipe to reach the house. Eureka—free gas and plenty of it.

When he'd told her about it she'd worried that the sheriff would come and arrest them for theft. But Eric had laughed and said that every living soul in the county did it and so did all the businesses.

And he was very nearly right.

The tapping took not very long at all and, though it was technically an act of theft it didn't have to be stealthily done under cover of darkness. In fact, owing to the multitude of derricks with flares burning constantly atop them, one would have been hard pressed to find a place in New London where it wasn't sufficiently well lit to read a newspaper even in the middle of a cloudless, moonless night.

Everybody knew the oil companies had no more use for the gas than to heat the boilers that ran the machinery at the rigs. Anything left over, which was a considerable amount, was free for the taking. So the men figured that if the fat cats didn't want it, they oughtn't look a gift horse in the mouth.

They also knew that the local police just didn't care that theft was being committed. The policemen themselves were doing the same thing.

The men also knew—at least some of them did—that the unrefined "green" or "wet" gas they were using was unstable, changing its properties constantly.

All Virgie Abercrombie knew, as she finished pinning the last of the laundry to the line, was that not having to pay a gas bill meant a little more leeway in a household budget that was stretched tight enough as it was.

Seven

Ardyth Davidson, Pearl Shaw, and Dorothy Womack settled into their seats in the auditorium along with the rest of the students in grades five through eleven. A few minutes had been whittled off the end of one period and a few more off the beginning of the next to allow time for a short assembly before the first of the academic and athletic teams climbed onto buses to travel to the county meet in Henderson.

Because this was something in the nature of a pep rally, with Superintendent Shaw as the sole cheerleader and pep squad, the various teams—for a plethora of events, everything from track and field and baseball to typewriting, slide rule, elocution, and debate—tried to sit together. There was considerable overlapping, of course, so individual students had to decide which group to raise their standard with, so to speak.

Ardyth was on the softball team and in the band. But she didn't think twice about choosing to sit instead with her best friends Pearl and Dorothy, who weren't on any team at all. The trio spent as much time together as they could manage.

They'd even found themselves a hidey-hole of sorts to eat their lunch in until a couple of weeks before. A storage room directly under the stage they were now facing was easily accessible through an unlocked door. The girls had located the room soon after the Christmas break and took their sandwiches or burgers down there every day to talk about things—mostly boys and movie stars—and enjoy their midday meal together.

The daily gathering continued until a teacher saw them coming out one day; that afternoon they were called to the office and told in no uncertain terms to never go there again. The almost immediate appearance of a big padlock on the door ensured that they would not disobey that edict.

A girl behind them leaned forward and asked where they'd been the night before when she'd telephoned. Dorothy said they'd all three gone to the roller-skating rink over in Overton, the three words delivered as one. They'd all worn something green, it having been Saint Patrick's Day, but not enough to discourage a little pinching, just in case some boys were there. One of their mothers had driven the three miles to deliver them and another had picked them up a couple of hours later.

When all of the students and teachers were in their seats Mr. Shaw, who was Pearl's uncle, walked slowly up onto the stage. His stiff necktie was pinched tight at his narrow neck as it always was, and his thick eyeglasses, reflecting the overhead stage lights, shone as brightly as headlamps on a car.

Ardyth whispered that she didn't think she'd have time to eat lunch with Pearl and Dorothy today. She planned to go by the office and pay her subscription to the *London Times*, the school paper published every Friday "by the Secretarial Training Class, to be concerned solely with news of interest to the student body." Last week's edition had run a list, typed out neatly in pale blue mimeograph ink and for the most part spelled correctly, of students who were in arrears. Her name was on it. Then she'd have to eat her sandwich quickly as she hurried out to the gym to change into her uniform and be back in time to take the team picture. Her coach had maintained that there wouldn't be time to take it after school, since they had to get on the bus and head off to Henderson for their game.

A teacher at the end of their row shushed her as Mr. Shaw adjusted the microphone. It squealed a little and then the room fell silent.

Assemblies were held often in the London school, and the students knew exactly how to behave in them. Mr. Shaw demanded that a speaker, be it himself or a third grader reciting a poem, be given the undivided attention of every member of the audience. Anything less than that might, and usually did, result in a student being removed from his or her seat and trotted up the aisle—"like a common criminal" one girl had famously said when she'd made the much-watched journey—to the office to await what they had coming to them, usually at the business end of a paddle.

So this morning Mr. Shaw spoke, after a prayer offered up by a sixth grader and the recitation of the Pledge of Allegiance led by a sophomore in his Boy Scout uniform, to a completely silent gathering of over five hundred people.

On some days, he began by reminding them of how fortunate they all were to be sitting in the finest high school auditorium in the state of Texas. Some days he would say the entire school was the finest, and some days—depending on the purpose of the assembly—he praised the library. Or the science labs, the stadium, or the domestic science building, consisting of a sewing room, a kitchen, a pantry, a formal dining room, a parlor, and even a bedroom.

But today he spoke only about the county meet. And of his gratitude for the hard work everyone had put in preparing for it and his faith in their ultimate success.

He ended by saying he was very proud of his boys and girls.

Which, even though only one young man in the big room was his actual offspring, was what he always called the many students in his charge.

Eight

Shortly after lunch, a group of fifth graders marched in single file behind their teacher out the back door of the building.

The PTA was meeting at three and these students, outfitted in large sombreros and multicolored ponchos over their regular clothes, needed to rehearse a Mexican hat dance they'd be doing for the ladies beforehand.

Since the routine the teacher had choreographed required that the dancers find their marks, the location of the meeting had been moved at the last minute from the auditorium, where the PTA always met, out to the gymnasium, a free-standing structure directly behind the main building, so that chalk lines could be drawn on the floor.

At three o'clock Marie Patterson, the superintendent's secretary, stepped into his office and said that the editor of the newspaper over in Henderson was on the telephone to interview him about tomorrow's meet. Mr. Shaw asked her to give him just a moment to look over the list of students who were participating before putting the call through.

He located the pad with the information but, rather than look at it, he swiveled around in his wooden chair and looked out the tall window for the first time since that morning.

The students in the elementary school, always released at three, a half hour before the junior high and high school, were leaving campus, heading home for a three day weekend. Mr. Shaw had just made his mandatory appearance before the PTA meeting commenced and watched some fifth graders stumble their way through some sort of dance involving big hats. The ladies were meeting in the gymnasium, so some of the elementary children were drifting back there to wait for their mothers.

He leaned back and enjoyed the good feeling that always came at the end of the school day. And this had been a particularly good one, with one of the best attendance records of the year so far. Almost all of his students had been counted present.

The heavy black phone on his desk rang and he lifted up the receiver.

≈

One hundred and twenty five miles away Walter Cronkite leaned back in a chair almost exactly like Mr. Shaw's and watched a quiet teletype machine in the Dallas bureau office of United Press International, willing it to send out something, anything, to break the monotony of the long afternoon.

He'd been sent down temporarily—"loaned out" they called it, as if he were a mystery novel or a garden implement—from the Kansas City bureau because of a shortage of personnel in Dallas. Which was fine with him. He was in his early twenties, not yet married, and he'd lived in Texas since he was ten. He'd done most of his growing up in Houston, had been the editor of his high school newspaper, majored in journalism at the University of Texas at Austin, and then hired on with UPI after graduating. So returning to Texas, albeit short-term, was something of a homecoming.

Cronkite's official title in Dallas was editor of the state wire, which meant he stayed in close proximity to the machine dedicated to that line.

The machine that sat, just then, quiet and unpromising.

He lifted a deck of playing cards out of the desk drawer. It was a few minutes past three. He leaned back in his chair and decided to play a couple of hands of solitaire before turning the wire machine off for the day.

Then he'd go back to his hotel.

Nine

In the library Pearl Shaw was licking postage stamps and putting them on notices to be mailed to parents of students who had overdue books. She and Dorothy Womack, both eighth graders, were assigned to the library during the final period every day.

The librarian, sufficiently devoted to her calling to recruit new priestesses, kept them busy shelving books, checking them out at the circulation desk, and keeping the card catalogue updated and correctly alphabetized.

The two friends liked working in the library well enough, but where they really wanted to be during this period was in Mr. Tate's science class with Ardyth Davidson. Mr. Tate had been the favorite teacher of the three girls in the junior high school, and had been moved up to high school—which required nothing more elaborate than carrying his few possessions from his old classroom to a different one at the opposite end of the building—when the girls had started the eighth grade. Ardyth had been lucky enough to be assigned to his class and Pearl and Dorothy, who hadn't, requested a schedule change. But Mr. Duran, the principal, had said no.

So here they were, doing the bidding of the librarian.

Neither girl was particularly interested in reading anything they didn't have to, other than the occasional movie magazine, but Pearl had recently put back a handsome edition of *Little Women* that she'd unpacked with some other volumes the librarian had sent away for.

The year before she'd heard some girls back in junior high talking about a character in the novel named Jo who had several sisters and might, from the sound of it, actually be a girl rather than a boy. She'd checked out the worn, yellowed copy that had surely been in the library of the old school before this one had been built and could, from the looks of it, have even predated the turn of the century. But she hadn't gotten past the first few pages. So she thought she'd have a go at this new one, with its sharp corners and colorful pictures.

She'd make sure she took it home with her in a little while.

≈

At the other end of the building, in Mrs. Wright's fifth grade English class, Bill Thompson's mind was occupied not a bit with the story the teacher was talking about but with Billie Sue Hall, whose dainty curls and wide smile had caught his attention that autumn and held on tight.

The problem was that there were several desks between Billy Sue and him, so he scribbled out a plea and handed it to Ethel Dorsey, the girl sitting behind the object of his young heart's desire.

When Mrs. Wright turned to write something on the blackboard, Ethel came back and motioned for Bill to take her seat. When he was in it, and smiling at Billie Sue, who was smiling back at him, he made a mental note to thank Ethel, who by her sacrifice had moved a little closer to the center of the room.

And away from the windows.

≈

Down the hall, eleven-year-old William Grigg was having trouble staying still in his desk in a big study hall that filled two classrooms and was overseen by several teachers. William was fidgety by nature and even more so at the end of the school day, when the call of the outside world beyond the tall, open windows was strong indeed.

He'd opened his speller and closed it again five or six times, had tapped his fingers along with the muted ticking of the clock over the blackboard, had drawn something roughly approximating a horse in his tablet, and finally he'd focused his attention on the bright afternoon. Out there, a couple of bobwhites sang to each other over the thumping of the oil rigs. Then a mockingbird chimed in until a crow, no respecter of good music, cawed loud enough to shut down the entire business.

Then the only sound in the big room was the clock and children turning pages and scraping the points of pencils and pens along paper. William watched the tops of green trees against blue sky and squinted his eyes almost shut to see if the colors would merge. They didn't. Then he began thinking about the shortcut through a wide pasture that he might or might not take on his way home. It didn't save him much time, that shortcut, but a pasture provided a more interesting journey than a road, and that particular pasture had a stock pond off to one side, under the shade of a giant cottonwood tree. The tank was hardly more than a large ditch, and always muddy, but it was a fine place to peel off and take a quick dip on a hotter day than this one, with enough banks — high mounds of sandy soil that had been bulldozed to make the pond — to provide some privacy.

His decision to go the road or the pasture would depend entirely on the mood of the bull that occupied the pasture. He had never actually charged at William, but the look in his eyes and the slow stomping of one hoof had indicated, more than once, that it had been on his mind.

Thinking about the bull caused him to begin squirming again and to shuffle his own feet on the floor. Then the teacher who was one of the keepers of the study hall during the last period of the day looked up from the papers she was grading and told him he was rolling around like a pig under a gate and to go next door to see if the teacher there needed any chores done. And to take the boy beside him along, since two wiry boys out of the room was better than one.

Ten

In the superintendent's outer office Mrs. Clarence Moore sat holding her purse in one of the hard, straight-backed chairs that were usually occupied by nervous students waiting to be called into The Presence. Her sister Marie Patterson, Mr. Shaw's secretary, was straightening the top of her desk before leaving for the day. Mrs. Moore had driven over to give her a ride home.

Mr. Shaw, having just finished his phone interview with the editor of the Henderson paper, came quickly out and wished the two ladies a good weekend. He'd been asked to referee a tennis match on the school courts that was supposed to have started at three.

He prided himself on being prompt in all things, and encouraged his faculty and students to do the same. So he hurried out of the office and out the front door of the school. He descended the steep steps, two at a time, pulling on his suit coat and slapping on his fedora.

~

Out in the gymnasium the ladies of the Parent Teacher's Association had worked their way through almost all of their agenda. Some of the children in the elementary grades who had already been released were trickling in to wait for their mothers to take them home.

The kids found some basketballs and started dribbling them around, the bouncing echoing off the high ceiling and walls of the big room. When they were shushed and then shushed again, the ladies finally suggested they go out and play on the big lawn in front of the school.

Some headed out there, but others turned their attention to whatever cookies were left on the refreshment table.

~

Dalton Abercrombie's teacher finished her lesson early and told her students they could switch seats if they wanted to and visit until the bell. Dalton got up and went to the back of the room and asked a girl if she wanted to trade so she could sit beside his friend.

He wondered where his older brother Boyd was this late in the day. Probably talking to anybody that would listen to him. He smiled, and hoped their mother would have something good in the way of a treat for them when they got home. She'd been talking about making teacakes for the last week or so, but she hadn't come up with any yet.

The girl Dalton had switched seats with turned around and smiled at him. She was a pretty thing, and had just recently risen in Dalton's estimation from an acquaintance to a candidate for something a little bit more than that.

She blushed. He blushed. His friend yakked on about fishing or hunting or something or other.

$\approx$

In Tyler, Mother Mary Ambrose counted once again through the neat, even stacks of printed programs for the next day's dedication ceremony in her office of the new Mother Francis Hospital, resplendent on its hilltop, which had yet to see a single patient.

The bishop and his staff world arrive soon from Dallas, and Mother Regina, the Provincial Superior, had already been collected at the train station and was getting a few minutes of rest after her journey.

Mother Ambrose could use a nap herself, as surely the sisters and nurses she'd watched work hard all day could. But there would be time enough, she figured, for resting tonight.

And they'd need their sleep. Tomorrow was the big day.

$\approx$

In Wright City, Floy Dees was rolling out dough on her kitchen counter. When she had it as close to paper thin as she could manage she sliced out long strips of dumplings that she carefully laid on wax paper dusted with flour. After a while she would lower them, one at a time, into the pot of chicken and broth already simmering on the stove.

That morning, she'd driven several miles over to her Uncle Chenault Barron's store in Henry's Chapel to buy fresh chicken and a few other things she needed. Barron's General Mercantile was well-known in the area for their specials, which usually didn't go into effect until Friday. This was a Thursday, but she'd known he would give her a discounted price on her purchases.

Marvin always told people she was a fine hand at making chicken and dumplings. And she was. She and her sister Sarah had been taught well by their mother when they'd been so little they'd had to stand on a chair to watch the procedure.

She wiped her hands on a dish towel and peeked into the pot and then at the perfectly aligned strips of dough waiting to go in. She opened the oven door only wide enough to see that the latticework crust on her peach pie was nearly perfectly brown.

She'd figured that as long as she had to roll out a batch of dough, she might as well use every smidgen of it.

Eleven

In front of the elementary school Charles Henry Erikson and his brothers, all three elementary students, were on their way home.

Their Sunday School teacher's house was just up the highway, and she was usually good for a glass of ice water or milk or maybe a cookie. They'd picked three coffee cans full of dewberries for her the weekend before, so maybe there would be a cobbler to show for it.

The woods were teaming with dewberry vines, and children who were brave enough to face the redbugs and the possibility of snakes could make a haul.

$\approx$

Janitor and bus driver Lonnie Barber waved at the Erikson boys as they walked by his parked bus in front of the elementary school. Then he nodded and smiled at the remainder of the first through fourth graders—who'd probably been kept after school to get a little extra help or a talking-to or a paddling— as they climbed on board. He knew them all by name, knew their families as well, and had grown up with many of their parents and their uncles and aunts.

They were chattering more than usual today, with the prospect of a three day weekend looming large.

Lonnie looked over at the junior high and high school, almost two hundred yards away, and wondered what his own four kids were up to this late in the day, not long before the final bell. Three of them would be participating in the big meet in Henderson tomorrow, so he figured they were working with their coaches and sponsors. He squinted and searched the windows, looking for his daughter. On some afternoons she came to a window and waved at him before he left on his run.

She wasn't there today.

He pulled the heavy lever that closed the bus door, found first gear with the tall shifter, and eased the bus out to the highway.

≈

By now William Grigg and his companion had reported to the teacher across the corridor from the study hall and been told to empty the trash can and collect the dirty erasers from the trays under the chalkboards and take them out and pound them against the wall to shake out the day's accumulation of chalk dust.

They made their way down the empty corridor, William cradling the erasers against his chest like pieces of kindling wood, the other boy hugging the metal garbage can. Their footsteps echoed off the double rows of metal lockers; the only other sound was the discordant assortment of muffled, pinging taps that came from the typing class, substantially quieter today because all of the really good typists had already left for the county meet.

It was almost as quiet, William thought, as it got in church when the singing was over and everybody got comfortable in the pews to wait for the preacher to stand up and launch into his sermon. At the rear door, William had to do a little balancing with the erasers to work the big handle. When it wouldn't depress, he thought it might be locked.

The other boy said they'd have to go out the front door. But William knew that Mr. Shaw had outlawed cleaning erasers anywhere but in the back since he had, on his way home one late afternoon, discovered an abstract spattering of white rectangles beside the handsome entrance to his school.

The taps of the faraway typewriters reverberated slowly along the hallway, as if they had found their way into the tiles of the floor, the metal doors of the lockers, the glass panes in the tall windows. William laid his cargo carefully on the floor and pulled harder on the door handle.

This time it gave way.

He scooped up the pile of erasers and the two boys moved through the open door into sunshine and fresh air.

Twelve

Four miles away, near Turnertown, on a cleared piece of land leased by the Texas Company, Marvin Dees wiped his brow and tossed a huge pipe wrench into the back of the crew truck.

He and his four companions had finished doing two days' worth of repairs and routine maintenance on a battery of three tanks, each with a capacity of five hundred barrels. A heady mixture of oil, gas, and water was piped from all the wells on that lease as soon as it surged up from ancient, underground lodes. Its baptism into the upper world was a sloshing run through the tanks, their manifolds, and finally separators, where the trio of properties would be divided and sent off in different directions. Some of the gas was vented directly into the atmosphere; the rest was pushed through other pipes to undergo a scrubbing before being routed back to the individual rigs to be either used to run the machinery or flared off. At least what was left to make the final journey, that is. Most of the regions' citizens and businesses had relieved the companies of much of the gas by then, to power their water heaters and furnaces and to fuel kitchen stoves and ignite gas lights.

Marvin dipped a tin cup of water from the can on the side of the crew truck and drank it all down in one long quaff. The other men were picking up the last of the tools and killing time before loading up and driving back to the company yard in Wright City. It was too late in the day to move to another lease and start a new job.

Marvin looked up at a golden sun in a cloudless sky. He guessed the time, flipped open his pocket watch to check himself, and hadn't missed it by much. A quarter past three.

The cool night and early morning had given way to a fine afternoon. He put the temperature at seventy, give or take a few degrees either way. Now that all the commotion of the work day—clanging and pounding and pulleys squealing and men shouting out to each other—was over he could actually hear a few birds singing out in the trees beyond the clearing. A crew from one of the other companies drove by on the highway and honked and waved.

Marvin waved back.

He was smart enough to know that he was too young to know much. But he knew that he could do this work, could do it as well or better than any other man. And he knew that as long as he had a job, and Floy waiting for him at home every afternoon, he could put himself down as lucky.

≈

As much as she liked Mr. Tate, Ardyth Davidson was beginning to think his science class would never end.

There had been no experiments today, just a short review of a chapter in the textbook during the first half of the period. Then Mr. Tate had said for everyone to complete the study questions in their notebooks.

Ardyth made a halfhearted attempt at the first couple, then put her pencil down and began playing the softball game in her mind that she would soon be playing on a field after a ten mile bus ride over to Henderson. She fiddled with the small, circular brooch on the coat her mother made her take along. The animal inside the ceramic circle looked sometimes like a racing horse and sometimes like a greyhound dog, depending on the angle.

The pretty afternoon spilled into the room through the open windows and Mr. Tate — young and handsome, newly married, and the father of the cutest baby Ardyth thought she'd ever seen — smiled in bright sunlight at a student in the front row. Ardyth curled one leg up under her and wished the last few minutes of the school day would magically dissolve so she could hurry out to meet the rest of her team at the bus.

She looked, one last time, at Mr. Tate, then at her folded coat and the brooch and its horse. Or dog.

≈

Boyd Abercrombie's final period teacher told him to stop talking so many times that she finally just let him open the floodgates for the last few minutes of class.

Other kids turned in their desks to listen to whatever yarn he was spinning. One girl asked how his little brother was doing in those big casts on his legs and Boyd told her that Talmage was such a spunky rascal that they didn't slow him down much. He actually stopped talking for a few seconds when he thought of his two-year-old brother and the teacher looked up from her grading to see if anything was wrong.

Then Boyd said that those casts had actually come in handy now and then, especially on windy days when they could prop Talmage against a door to keep it from blowing shut.

Everybody laughed at that, even the teacher.

But she shut the show down when Boyd started singing.

≈

Sibyl Jordan, a seventh grader, was certain that she'd been told that the last period wouldn't meet today because of the PTA meeting in the gym.

So when the bell had rung ending the next to the last period she'd hurried out of the building and come out to her bus. The driver could have set her straight and turned her around if he'd been there, but most of the drivers were teachers or janitors who didn't get to the buses until the kids did.

She watched, through the bus window, elementary students milling around between their building and the bigger school. The total absence of anyone older than a fourth grader outside left no doubt that she had made a mistake. If she'd just looked in the open window of her last period class as she'd walk past it and seen it full of kids she wouldn't have been counted absent. She'd have been where she was supposed to be.

Sibyl liked to be where she was supposed to be.

She considered going back in and enduring the stares and giggles she would get by showing up late, then she pulled a library book out of her satchel and settled back against the seat to wait for the day to be finished and the bus to fill up with students, her sister Mildred, a ninth grader, among them. Their younger sister Billie, an elementary student, had stayed home today.

By now Sibyl was tired of reading, and figured it surely couldn't be long before the final bell rang, so she packed her book away. When one of her teachers walked quickly across the lawn she leaned out the window and shouted that she had something to tell her. But the teacher called back that she was late for a meeting and hurried on to the front of the school, up the steps, and into the front entrance.

Sibyl watched the heavy white doors close slowly behind her, and wished she had stopped. Because what she had wanted to tell her was important.

But try as she might, from time to time over the next seventy years or so, she would never be able to recall what it was.

Thirteen

Behind the school Doris Shoemate, who had completely forgotten the argument she'd had with her mother early that morning, much less its origin, was walking up the steps leading to the back door at the southeastern corner.

She and two friends had been out to the gymnasium to deliver a note from a teacher to one of the PTA ladies.

It certainly didn't take three seventh grade girls to deliver one small slip of paper, but this late in the day they were as anxious to move around as their teacher was to let them do it.

Doris giggled at whatever one of the other girls said, reached for the handle, and pulled the heavy door toward her.

≈

Lemmie Butler, a manual arts instructor, inspected a recently repaired portable sander that sat on a bench beside the door at the rear of his shop.

Because of the slant of the long hill that fell away behind the building, the shop and several other classrooms were located in sections beneath the two rear wings.

Butler always left the back door open for easy access to stacks of lumber, used for student projects, which were stored just inside the vast crawl space that was two hundred and fifty-three feet long, fifty-six feet wide, with an average height of four and a half feet, depending on the level of the earth floor. All of it comprised an area that ran under the concrete floor of most of the school building.

And all of it was filled, at that moment, with almost sixty five thousand cubic feet of odorless natural gas.

Butler flipped the electrical switch over the door to check the sander.

It threw a spark.

≈

Eyewitnesses would always—even as very old people many, many years later—remember different details in different ways.

But on one point, there was a clear consensus.

The London school, at the moment that it exploded, lifted up off the ground to a height of several feet. Before the walls sucked themselves in and then swelled out in massive broken pieces, before the roof collapsed, before the gigantic cloud of dust billowed up into the blue afternoon sky, the long building, still complete, rose up for what seemed to more than a few of the witnesses longer than it was physically possible for it to sustain its levitation.

Some of them wondered, in fact, in that elongated few seconds of surreal horror, if it might just keep rising up and up.

And never come down again.

Part Two

Like Somebody Had Lifted the Lid off a Kettle

Fourteen

It was the floor—eight inches of solid cement resting on over one hundred concrete piers emerging from platforms buried an average of three feet underground—that propelled the building into its short-lived flight.

When the school was built the outer walls were poured as a single unit, making the inadequately vented crawl space beneath the slab virtually a sealed compartment. So when the gas exploded, the floor went in the only direction it could, which was up. It initially held together, supporting the building intact for the few seconds that would burn themselves irrevocably into eyewitnesses' memories, before breaking into massive juggernauts of concrete, brick, and twisted steel reinforcement rods, all of which tore through everything in its path. Through walls and ceiling and roof.

And people.

There were, at 3:17 on Thursday afternoon, March 18, 1937, approximately five hundred students and forty teachers in the building that housed the junior high and high schools. A definite number would never be agreed upon. Some of the pupils and a few teachers had already left for the county meet, some kids had surely played hooky on a pretty afternoon before a three day weekend, and any attendance records, which would have been tabulated by Mr. Shaw's secretary Marie Patterson earlier in the afternoon, perished in the blast.

As did Miss Patterson herself, along with her sister Mrs. Clarence Moore, who was waiting to give her a ride home. Both were killed, either when the floor exploded beneath them or the walls and ceiling and roof rained down on them.

In the general science room Ardyth Davidson died in her softball uniform, still holding the coat her mother had made her bring to school. Mr. Tate, the teacher, was also killed, as were all the students in the room except for two.

The brooch on Ardyth's coat was broken nearly in half, its horse or dog now incomplete but still in a full-out run, like an image frozen in time on the

Grecian urn in Keats' ode. The brooch and what was left of the coat would eventually be packed carefully away by Ardyth's parents.

Later.

After the initial horror and the scrambling for survivors and for bodies or parts of bodies.

After the several hundred funerals.

≈

Later, when all the dire tallying would be completed, it would become quickly apparent that most of the deaths occurred in the rooms on the long hallway that ran the entire length of the front section of the school. That portion of the building, roughly three quarters of the whole, sat exactly over the crawl space where the gas had collected and exploded.

Directly north of the room where Mr. Tate and Ardyth Davidson died was Miss Katie Mae Watson's English class at the school's northwest corner. Miss Watson and all but five of her students were killed. Next door, at the north end of the hallway, only four of Mr. Bunch's math students survived. Across the hall from Mr. Tate's science class were two large typing and bookkeeping classrooms. Many of the typing students were already in Henderson for the meet; all who remained behind were killed.

A big auditorium took up much of the center of the building, its front doors facing the main entryway. Though it was by far the largest room in the place it was, at 3:17, occupied by only two people. Lucille Walker, a student, had just been given a music lesson on the stage by Miss Queenie Price, a music teacher who worked part time for the school. Lucille survived the blast, but would be hospitalized for several months after being extracted, early the next morning, from the ruins. Her mother, who had come in to watch the lesson and was helping Lucille gather her things to go home, was killed. Miss Price, the music teacher, died in the teacher's lounge near the front entrance while waiting to give a piano lesson.

Adjacent to the auditorium to the south were two classrooms filled with between sixty and seventy students that comprised a massive study hall overseen by several teachers. All of them died except for William Grigg and another boy who had been sent outside to clean erasers and empty a trash basket.

Opposite the study hall were the rooms of Mr. J. H. Propes, who died with all thirty of his arithmetic students, and Mr. Louis Waller, who died alone grading papers at his desk during his planning period.

The southernmost rooms, where the hall made a western turn toward the outside doors leading to the gymnasium, were an English class and, at the southwest corner, an art and penmanship class taught by Miss Laura Bell. Of the sixty or so students in those rooms all but a dozen died.

The main entryway was at the center of the front of the school, between the front doors and the entrance to the auditorium. Next to the entryway were the offices of the superintendent, Mr. Shaw, who was hurrying out to the tennis courts to officiate a match, and high school principal Troy Duran, who was already in Henderson for the county meet. The outer office—where teachers came to get their mail or use the telephone and where students were sent to await whatever punishment lay in store for them—was where Miss Patterson and her sister Mrs. Moore died, probably looking at each other across Miss Patterson's desk.

It wouldn't have been the worst way to die, some would say later. Looking directly at someone who loved and cared about you, and was about to accompany you on the journey.

Fifteen

The rear sections that comprised the trio of horizontal extensions of the E-shaped building, not built over the crawl space but on solid ground, did not collapse.

In the library, at the northeast corner, Dorothy Womack had been stamping a check-out card one moment, and the next she was on her back under the circulation counter with more furniture and chunks of wall and ceiling all around her than she figured she'd ever be able to dig herself out of.

She remembered that Pearl had just been standing right beside her, saying how she needed to run down to the office to get more penny postcard stamps to affix to notices of overdue library fines that would be mailed on Monday. Dorothy had volunteered to go with her, since running up and down the halls was a favorite activity of freshmen girls.

Dorothy had no idea how she'd ended up in her current predicament, or where Pearl was, or the boy she was about to hand the library book to, or if either of them were even alive after whatever had happened . . . happened.

A tall steel filing cabinet was wedged uncomfortably close to her, leaving her little in the way of wiggle room. One gentle push at its cold surface confirmed that it was the reason her small space wasn't filled up with debris.

Kids were screaming in the reading room, which adjoined the library. And somebody—Joe King, she thought, an eleventh grader—was yelling at them not to go down the stairwell.

Dorothy realized that she wouldn't be going down a stairwell or anywhere else in the foreseeable future. She ran her hand along the slick surface of the providential file cabinet and wondered how long it would be able to hold back the massive weight of rubble on top of it before it shifted.

The kids in the reading room, and others further away, were still screaming. So she did too.

≈

Whoever Dorothy heard shouting about the stairwell had a good reason. In the frantic confusion he was perhaps the only person who, rather than going into shock or closing his eyes against the horror or scrambling wildly for any exit he could find, looked up. He saw a section of dislodged concrete the size of an automobile hanging precariously over the stairs like a big boulder waiting to fall from a cliff's edge.

He figured the massive thing would crash down soon. Of course, he thought, as he continued to yell out his warning, the whole place might topple first.

Gravity would be victorious, one way or another, sooner or later.

≈

Next door to the library, English teacher Miss Lizzie E. Thompson had been telling her tenth graders about the life of Poe when the building rumbled and shook and the side of the room that adjoined Mr. Bunch's math class fell completely away.

Only five of her twenty-two students survived. One of them, Corene Gary, would always remember the three words—*Jesus help us*—that Miss Thompson silently mouthed just before she was engulfed by the crashing wall.

John Fuhr—a lanky blonde boy with a clear, carefully paced, and confident orator's voice that would serve him well the next day in front of newsreel cameras and decades later when recalling the tragedy—tried to help his classmates who might still be alive, stepping quickly over those that obviously weren't.

And most of them, he soon discovered, weren't.

≈

William Grigg and the other boy who'd been sent out with him to empty the wastepaper basket and clean erasers hadn't gotten very many feet away from one of the back doors of the building when the earth gave a violent shake, erasers erupted out of William's tight embrace like a covey of startled quail, and he fell to the ground.

From there he couldn't see the other boy, and never would again. But what he did see would stay with him forever.

The entire front section of the school had seemed to float for a few long seconds in midair before suddenly sucking its walls in and then, just as suddenly, pushing them out again before bursting into countless pieces and crashing down.

William's first impulse was to run.

And it seemed an excellent time to follow a first instinct.

So he sprinted toward the tall fence at the back of the school property. He'd tried to climb that very fence several times with his friends. But he never could.

Until today.

Sixteen

The first people to arrive were the mothers who had been in their PTA meeting in the gymnasium behind the main building. The blast had been strong enough to knock most of them out of their chairs and almost all of the window panes out of their casements, sending broken glass cascading down to the bleachers and the floor. By the time the women ran out the front door the dust was so thick they could barely make out the back of the three rear sections of the school and, between them, the entire main mass of the building still falling in on itself, its tiled roof crashing down at the last.

Some of the women collapsed where they'd stopped to take it all in. Others ran toward the first piles of debris they came to and started pulling heavy clods of brick and roofing away with their bare hands.

Because the initial horror quickly gave way to an even more horrible reality.

Their children were inside. Somewhere.

So they dug.

≈

Five miles away at the Texas Company lease south of Turnertown, Marvin Dees and the crew he worked with had heard the muffled explosion and might or might not have felt the ground tremble slightly. There would be some disagreement about that.

Marvin's first thought, which he wouldn't remember speaking aloud, was that a boiler had exploded at one of the rigs. One of the other men shook his head and said it was too loud for that, too big, that maybe somebody was using dynamite on one of the leases. Everyone started talking at once and then the men stood quietly by their truck and watched a thick cloud of dark dust climb up into the sky beyond a stand of pines.

As they hurled the last of their tools clattering into the truck's bed somebody screeched to a stop on the highway, just down the hill. The driver yelled up at them in frantic snatches of sentences. "New London . . . everything . . . the school . . . Jesus! . . . You fellers got any first aid stuff?"

Every crew truck of every company was supposed to have a first aid kit on board. Theirs actually did. When Marvin found it he held it up for the other men to see, like an offering to—or a confirmation of—what they were about to do. Whatever it might turn out to be.

The men looked again at the cloud that had billowed up even higher and was beginning to fall apart at its edges.

Then they scrambled into the truck and raced toward New London.

≈

Mr. Shaw had almost made it to the tennis courts to officiate a match when his school exploded. He'd been knocked down by the initial blast and then struck in the head by a piece of flying debris.

He might have blacked out for a moment, but was back on his feet soon and making his wobbly way toward . . . what? He couldn't think of a specific place he should head for, since nothing seemed to be where it had been just a few moments before. The place where his office should be was now just a pile of bricks and broken cement, dust rising off it like thick smoke from a fire. He lost his balance and fell, then someone helped him up and tied something around his head and handed him his hat.

Townspeople quickly hurried onto the campus, and people who had been driving down the highway. Nobody seemed to know what to do except stand in awe of the unimaginable destruction. Some began to pull the frantically digging mothers away from their task; others fell to their knees and helped them.

When the makeshift bandage had been tied to Mr. Shaw's bleeding head, he pointed helplessly all around him and muttered for the first time the slow mantra that he would repeat all through the long afternoon and night.

"There are children in there," he mumbled. "My boys and girls are in there."

Seventeen

L onnie Barber had driven his bus past the front of the school, turned on to a dirt road, then shifted down into low gear to start the slow climb up a long hill. Just before the top, the ground shook, the very air outside the open windows rumbled, and all of his elementary passengers scrambled to the back and began to scream. He pulled to a stop and told everyone to get back in their seats, speaking loud enough so they would look at him and not out the back window.

Many of the kids were crying, and some were shouting out names of brothers or sisters who were in the junior high and high school. Barber had to restrain several of the boys to keep them from getting off the bus.

Some of the kids were hysterical; some were in shock. He didn't know how to aid or comfort either sort, and he figured the only thing for him to do was to get these kids away from whatever had happened.

He knew he needed to get them home.

He also knew, as he moved the bus forward, that his own four children were in the building that was at the bottom of the mass of dark dust that filled up his rearview mirror.

≈

By the time Marvin Dees and his crew reached town the long front façade of the school was nothing more than a swirling cauldron of dust, and more piles of rubble than Marvin would have ever thought possible. Parts of the two rear wings and the back of the big auditorium, two stories tall owing to the steep downward slope of a hill, were still standing. But fragments of their walls continued to slide free and crash down, one piece at a time.

Desks and parts of chalkboards dangled unsteadily at the jagged edges of the second story flooring, just beyond which Marvin could make out, through the floating dust, people slowly milling around up there.

≈

William Grigg ended up climbing the fence twice that had previously proven to be insurmountable.

Once on the other side he'd heard the PTA mothers screaming and then people in the ruined building joining in. William's two older brothers were in there somewhere. And the thought that one or both of them might be doing some of the caterwauling, or that they needed his help, had stopped him in his tracks.

So he'd scaled the fence again.

By the time he'd nearly lost his voice shouting out their names and had pulled away what seemed like a ton of debris, so many people had arrived that he knew that finding Edwin and Horace in all the confusion was unlikely at best, and probably impossible.

One of the last cadavers he saw, before altering his plan, was just the head and shoulders of a girl in his class.

He stopped and looked at what was left of her for a long moment and tried to recall her name. He knew it well enough, since he sat close to her every day in a couple of classrooms. But it wouldn't come. Maybe, William thought, something as meaningful as a name couldn't be easily associated with the grotesque thing on the ground. Then he decided to go where things made more sense.

He took a deep breath, and started walking toward home.

≈

When Pearl Shaw got to her feet she was standing, not in the library where she'd just been with Dorothy Womack, but in what had been the hallway that led to the main section of the building. Now it stretched just a few yards before falling off into nothingness. Or, more precisely, into the particles of dust and brick and concrete and shingles that still danced around in midair.

It took her a few minutes to get her bearings. And another two or three for the popping in her ears to die down enough to let her make out Dorothy's voice among countless others.

She tried to call out her name, but discovered that her mouth and throat were filled with concrete dust. So until she could ether spit some of it up or swallow it, one proposition about as impossible at the moment as the other, she realized that when it came to verbal communication she was as mute as an unplugged radio.

≈

Elbert Shoemate, the baby of the family that included Sammie, aged ten, and Doris, twelve, had had what amounted to a front row seat for the explosion.

His third grade class had been released with the rest of the elementary school at three. Less than twenty minutes later he stood outside and watched what he would later describe as the big building going up in one piece and coming back down, mighty fast, in chunks.

Which was not something that a third grader, or anybody else for that matter, was likely to see very often.

The Shoemates lived in a shotgun house owned by the Spansco Oil Company, Mr. Shoemate's employer, three miles up the Henderson highway. Elbert would always swear he ran the entire distance. Perhaps he did. He was a strong runner, and especially so when he was in a race or wanted badly to get someplace.

Today he just wanted to get to where his mother was.

Eighteen

M arvin Dees quickly came to the sick realization that the small first aid kit he had clutched so tightly that his fingers had gone white would be of no help whatsoever.

The first thing he and the other roughnecks did was to try to get the mothers away from their gruesome business. Men who were not usually given to speaking softly did so now. "Let me do this now, Ma'am. You go right over there and let me do this. I can do it faster, you see."

People from the town were there now, the womenfolk trying to pull the screaming PTA mothers away. But most were persistent, and wouldn't go. Fathers were rushing in now, pushing people and things out of their way and pulling away concrete. Much of the rubble was, of course, too large and too heavy to be moved until machinery could be brought in. But desperate men pulled at it anyway, heaving until their lungs were near to bursting and their hands were bleeding.

They found body after body under the things they could lift. If someone was alive they picked them up and carried them out toward the highway. If they were dead, which they usually were, they left them and kept on looking. Unless it was their own child, of course. From time to time a sorrowful cry would go up and everyone knew that some father or mother, or both digging in tandem, had located their own son or daughter.

By unspoken agreement, prioritization became the rule; a system not unlike a triage scheme used in emergency rooms and by battlefield medics fell quickly into place where the dead were left where they were until the living were accounted for. The wounded were taken to cars and pickups and oil company crew trucks, though nobody knew where to take them once they were loaded.

Nobody knew, in fact, what to do about anything. Nobody had a plan. Nobody was in charge. The mayor of Henderson, the county seat ten miles away, soon arrived and, since New London was not yet an incorporated town and had no mayor, thought he should attempt some sort of coordination. He knew—and was no doubt thankful—that he would relinquish any responsibility soon enough, when others would arrive: state troopers, Texas Rangers, National Guardsmen, maybe even the governor. It would just be a matter of time, the mayor knew.

And that was good. Because the swarming mob of people he'd found when he arrived was growing by the minute. And they wouldn't be easily corralled into a plan of action.

Not that he had even the foggiest notion of what such a plan should entail.

Nineteen

B y the time Pearl Shaw located Dorothy Womack and assessed her situation she'd managed to dislodge and cough up enough cement dust to ask
her if she was hurt.

Dorothy, trapped under the library circulation desk with only the big file
cabinet fending off a deluge of heavy debris, told her she didn't really know.
Then Pearl put her hands through the lone hole, about the size of a canta-
loupe, in the rubble and started pulling things away. And in a few minutes
she'd managed to pull out Dorothy herself.

While her friend found her balance, brushed off dust, and stretched
some life back into her limbs, Pearl looked around at dead people, injured
people, more dead people, and what remained of a building that was still
in the process of collapsing, one big piece at a time. The huge mass of concrete still dangled precariously over the stairwell on a couple of strands of
twisted steel that looked about as fragile as hair ribbons. And the hallway
that had always led down to the main part of the building stopped abruptly
now in midair, since there was, simply enough, no longer a main part of the
building.

Something—the floor or the wall or maybe the injured soul of the place
itself, she couldn't tell which—commenced a low, pitiful moaning and more
things fell, sending the dust that was everywhere billowing up. Pearl watched
the dust swirl around in a wide band of sunlight and then looked up at its
source, a gaping hole in the ceiling very close to a pile of collapsed wall.

She grabbed Dorothy's hand and, leaning over far enough so she could
be heard over the din of screaming, crying children, told her they had to
get out.

With her other hand she pointed in the only direction she thought they
might accomplish it.

Up.

≈

Dorothy Shoemate woke up a good fifty feet away from the school's back door that she vaguely remembered pulling open. She couldn't be sure if she had or not.

She shook her head and reached up to find something tied around it. Her hand was bloody when she looked at it. If she couldn't be sure about going through the door—which hung awkwardly now by only its top hinge, putting it at cross-purpose to how it ought to fit—she certainly couldn't be sure how her hand had gotten bloody.

All of a sudden she just didn't seem to know anything. Except that she was sitting on the ground looking at the remnants of something so unexpected and horrible that she couldn't quite take it in or make any sense of it. And she knew that somebody was doing something to the back of her dress.

She looked around long enough to see that a man was tying the fabric to-gether that had been ripped or torn, undoubtedly, she knew as she looked again at the misshapen door, in her journey from over there to over here.

The man, who she knew was a roughneck because her father worked in the oil fields and she'd known roughnecks all her life, worked as gently as he could at the knot he was tying and told her to sit still for a minute.

So she sat still.

Twenty

Within minutes of the explosion, a teacher who had been in one of the outbuildings rushed to Mr. Shaw's house, found the telephone, and called the operator in Overton. The school was destroyed, he told whoever he was connected to, trying hard to keep his voice steady so that he would be understood over the line, and someone who could provide police and ambulances, and plenty of them, must be contacted immediately.

Another school employee drove quickly to the Western Union telegraph office, also in Overton. A. H. Huggins, the lone clerk there, sent a message, its importance deceptive in its brevity but enormous in its content, to his supervisor in Houston:

> An explosion at the New London school here . . . flash the news to the offices in this vicinity asking that they send doctors, nurses, and ambulances at once!

Mr. Huggins would have done well to have stretched then, and caught his breath. For his office would soon become a beehive of activity, sending messages for days and weeks to come, and receiving them from places both close by and as far away as the capitals of the world.

≈

Virgie Abercrombie had put a plate of teacakes, hot from the oven, on the kitchen table and was pouring the mugs of hot cocoa for Boyd and Dalton when the house shook and something erupted outside, almost like a distant roll of thunder.

Now, several minutes later, she watched from her front porch as her neighbors from other oil company shotgun houses hurried down toward the road, some of them crying, one or two screaming.

A single word—*school*—sputtered through the throng like an electrical current.

Virgie grabbed up two-year-old Talmage, still groggy from his nap, and swung his legs in their heavy casts around to ride on her hip as she bolted out the front door and off the porch to join the general stampede.

The puppy that had been snoring beside Talmage yapped once or twice at the commotion, yawned, and went back to sleep.

≈

In the United Press International office in Dallas Walter Cronkite, who had lingered over his last game of solitaire longer than he'd intended to, put the cards away in their pack, tightened his necktie, grabbed his hat, and reached over to turn off the teletype machine designated as the State Wire.

Suddenly it emitted three short, sharp rings. Then a furious tapping commenced and a brief message marched across its paper in all capital letters:

DO NOT CLOSE THIS WIRE!

The young reporter took off his fedora, sailed it toward the hat rack, loosened his tie, rolled his chair over to the teletype machine, and waited for its next spasm of activity.

≈

By the time Virgie Abercrombie and her neighbors got to what was left of the school injured students and teachers that could be freed by hand were being carried to pickups and cars parked end to end almost a mile along the highway and others that had honked their way though the quickly growing crowd on the wide lawn at the front of the campus.

Nothing in the way of a plan of action had yet materialized, so the drivers, knowing that their cargo needed medical attention and needed it fast, took off for Henderson and Kilgore and Jacksonville, where there were doctors with treatment rooms, and to Tyler, where there were a couple of small hospitals and, somebody said, a bigger one that hadn't opened yet.

Twenty-One

The abundance of chalky dust that had first been propelled upward in a massive cloud had found its way back to earth. Now it moved around like a living thing, but a confused one, slithering through the chaos of frantic humans and piles of rubble as if searching for where it was supposed to be.

Marvin Dees and his crew discovered early on that by moving debris off bodies and putting it somewhere else, it would just have to be moved again when they dug there. So somebody suggested they start toting the rubble that was small enough to be carried to the edge of the school campus, where it would be out of the way and wouldn't have to be constantly shuffled around.

All operations of the various oil companies drilling in the area had been shut down completely by now, and someone said that if some of the rough-necks who were rapidly spilling in could be put to work handing out chunks of rubble from hand to hand it would be speedier than each man trudging way out there and then back again.

Then providence supplied a small blessing amid the grisly chaos.

One of the many vehicles that stopped on the highway was a flatbed truck owned by a basket factory carrying a full load of hundreds of brand new peach baskets, each a foot and a half in diameter and about that deep, made of slats of curved thin wood with wire handles. They were quickly offloaded and put into service in relay lines, the equivalent of water bucket brigades at a house fire. The many baskets were filled with wreckage and sent hand to hand from the ruins of the demolished building out far enough to where there would be no bodies or buried survivors.

Then they were emptied and sent quickly back in again, in a process that would continue without pause for many hours.

~

Elbert Shoemate threw the front door open and collapsed in the first chair he came to. He'd covered the three miles between the school and his house in short order, running most if not all of it, only to discover that his mother wasn't there.

When he caught his breath and drank a glass of water he determined she'd probably gotten word about the explosion and had hurried there to find his sisters, Doris and Sammie, and himself. He probably had missed seeing their car on the highway because he'd taken some short cuts along the way.

Elbert knew he didn't have enough steam left to run back to town, or even walk there. The family didn't have a telephone, so he scribbled out a note saying he was okay and left it on the kitchen table. Then he headed for his uncle's house because he didn't want to be by himself.

And because it was considerably closer than three miles.

≈

Sibyl Johnson had watched the school explode mere seconds after the teacher that she had so wanted to tell something to had disappeared into the front door.

When the bus she was sitting on, otherwise empty but for her, stopped rocking from the blast, she got up, opened the front door, and took the first steps into her small chapter, unique in its simplicity, in the tremendously larger saga that was unfolding all around her.

Sibyl hurried around bodies and piles of debris and more bodies and bits of bodies and finally reached one of the rear sections that remained standing. The inside wall of what she knew was her sister Mildred's classroom had either fallen away or been pulverized in the explosion. And there, standing with some other bruised and tattered children, was Mildred, looking little the worse for wear.

Sibyl called up to her to climb down.

She did. And they walked home.

≈

Dalton Abercrombie was a bloody mess by the time he got to his house.

Bits of concrete had clung to his scalp, face, neck, and arms, sending blood in slow but steady rivulets down to his shirt and even his trousers.

On any other day if he had walked through town looking like he'd fallen under a hay mower everyone who saw him would have rushed to his aid. Today he'd managed to complete the trip with no interruptions. Today he'd blended in perfectly with several hundred other kids.

He took one look at the plate of untouched teacakes and the two mugs of cocoa that had gone cold and realized that his mother must have taken Talmage and hurried over to the school with what had seemed, from the size of the crowd when he'd left, what every other person in this county and a few others had done.

Talmage's puppy had had an accident on the floor, so he let him out before he had another one. Then he vacillated between cleaning himself up and changing his bloody clothes or going directly back to locate his family.

Before he made up his mind he remembered he hadn't seen his brother Boyd in the mass confusion. And Boyd, tall and loud and always talking, generally always stood out. Even in a crowd.

Without so much as changing his blood-soaked shirt, he headed back to the school, leaving the screen door slapping behind him.

≈

Pearl started up the pile of collapsed wall with the determination of a mountain goat, pulling Dorothy, as unsure of her footing as she was of where they were going, along behind her.

At the top they clung to each other and to the most stationary chunks of rubble to keep their balance as smaller bits shifted and tumbled down. When things had subsided a little, the girls made their way up through the opening and sat down near the edge of the roof.

Being out was a relief; the sunshine felt good. But one look down from their tall second-story perch at the jagged sections of concrete and brick wall on the ground made them wonder if they were really any better off than they had been inside.

Their doubts were confirmed when several red roof tiles, as if on cue, broke loose and clattered beside them before plummeting to the ground, which looked to be an awfully long way down.

Twenty-Two

In the Executive Mansion, across the street from the state capitol in Austin, Governor James V. Allred had cleared his appointments calendar for the day and was either taking a nap or strongly considering taking one when he was told of the disaster.

The preceding day and night had been long ones, culminating with his wife Joe Betsy giving birth to a healthy son, Sam Houston Allred, named not only for the hero of the Texas Revolution but for the birthing room itself, which had been Houston's bedroom when he had been governor. In fact, the new arrival had been born in the very bed in which one of the great man's own children had made her entrance into the world.

Governor Allred immediately did two things when he got the news: order the state police and Texas Rangers to New London and, as all good politicians are apt to do, have one of his minions draft an official statement to be put quickly into the hands of reporters.

Allred was a competent, though lackluster, governor sandwiched between two of the most memorable characters to ever hold office. His predecessor was Miriam Amanda "Ma" Ferguson, the first woman state chief executive in Texas and only the second in the nation, who had actually served two separate terms: 1925 to 1927 and 1933 to 1935. She'd first been elected after her husband, Governor James Edward Ferguson, had been impeached, convicted of taking bribes and misappropriation of public funds, ousted, and barred from ever again holding public office. The verdict had not, however, forbidden his wife from running. Her chief, and very nearly only, campaign promise had been that if elected she would closely follow all of the advice of her husband, thus giving Texans "two governors for the price of one."

Ma Ferguson was a somber, middle-aged lady seldom given to smiling (at least when having her photograph taken), who wore her hair usually in a bun and was not often seen in public in anything but matronly print dresses and sensible shoes. She was a nondrinker who railed against prohibition on

economic grounds, and was widely suspected, but never convicted, of award-
ing highway contracts only to companies that advertised in the newspaper
owned by her husband. Though she might never have actually said, when
asked her opinion regarding the teaching of foreign languages in the schools,
"If English was good enough for Jesus Christ, it should be good enough for
the children of Texas," it has been most often attributed to her, and has worked
its way into the uniquely rich mythology of the Lone Star state.

She also made famously good chili. Will Rogers was a frequent guest at the
governor's mansion during her terms, once skipping dessert so he could have
a fourth bowl of her specialty.

Allred would be succeeded by Pappy Lee O'Daniel, the president of the
Burris Mill and Elevator Company, which sponsored a wildly popular radio show starring a band called the Light Crust Doughboys. O'Daniel was
the personable host of the program, which consisted of country music interspersed with lively bantering aimed at selling the company's flour. The
Doughboys, one of them a formerly unknown singer named Bob Wills, were
household names in the Southwest, and O'Daniel would eventually float on
their popularity straight into Texas' highest office to the hokey hosannas of
hillbilly tunes.

Allred knew that the New London explosion would be front page news
across the nation, maybe around the world, in a few hours. So here, amid
great tragedy, was an opportunity for him to prove himself a strong leader.
He'd served with countless others in the Navy during the world war, worked
his way up inconspicuously though a series of political appointments, had
lost his first run for attorney general and won the next one, then had ridden
the coattails of President Roosevelt and his New Deal into the governor-
ship.

What he needed was a solo turn in the spotlight. And fate, it seemed, had
supplied just such an opportunity.

Almost a thousand miles away in Warm Springs, Georgia, the man to
whom Allred was almost religiously devoted, Franklin Roosevelt, had just
finished dedicating a new school for black children in a nearby town, and had
returned to the comfortable bungalow that the press had recently taken to
calling the Little White House. When he was given the news from Texas he
leaned forward in his wheelchair as he did at about the same time every afternoon and mixed a batch of dry martinis on the drink trolley, his mind working as carefully and confidently through what must first be done regarding

this new crisis as his hands did as they manipulated crystal decanters of gin and vermouth, a bowl of cracked ice, and a silver cocktail shaker.

By the time he'd tilted his icy concoction into several chilled glasses for the men in the room, he'd determined to basically do the same two things that his disciple in the governor's mansion in Texas was doing. He waved his long cigarette holder at someone and told them to get the Red Cross boys into action and to locate somebody in government, hopefully with a medical background, that was close enough to get to that school tonight and get him on the telephone. Somebody else was sent over to a typewriter to begin cobbling together a press release.

It was soon determined that one of the president's medical advisors was in Louisiana, where he was conducting some sort of health inspection. A wire was dispatched instructing him to go as quickly as possible to New London, which would first involve someone finding out exactly where it was. As it turned out, it was not a long journey for the doctor, since just one county stood between the site of the explosion and the Texas–Louisiana border.

Within an hour, a carefully worded statement was released by the president and handed out to the small army of reporters who made up his press entourage. In it he expressed his shock at the news of the deaths of hundreds of school children, making sure he used the name of not only the town but the state, since New London alone would make people think it happened in Connecticut. He also expressed his hope that further bulletins would lessen the scope of the tragedy and said he'd asked the Red Cross and all government agencies to render every assistance in their power.

When the brief epistle had been distributed the president, figuring he had done all he could do regarding that situation, probably drained the last of his drink, pushed a fresh cigarette into his holder, and shifted gears in his mind to something else. Perhaps Japanese aggression in Northern China. Perhaps the sluggish economy that wasn't showing much sign of recovery. Perhaps his second attempt to pack the Supreme Court.

Twenty-Three

George and Jessie Grigg assumed that a boiler had blown up on one of the leases when they heard the muffled explosion while having their afternoon coffee.

When their boy William hurried through the kitchen door a while later, babbling something about cleaning erasers and climbing fences and only the top half of a girl laying on the ground, they realized they'd been mistaken.

It took a while to settle him down enough for him to tell them what had happened. Then Jessie went to the door and looked down the road to see if William's brothers Edwin and Horace were on their way home.

Suddenly George was moving past her, putting on his hat and telling her to stay put in case they showed up.

William fell in behind him and announced that he was going too.

George said he'd best stay with his mother.

This didn't slow William down any. He kept his eyes focused on the road when he said again, to nobody in particular, that he was going too.

On the roof of what remained of the library Pearl and Dorothy waved their arms and screamed until their throats felt like sandpaper. Pearl's throat, because of all the concrete dust she'd had to deal with, had in fact already felt like sandpaper. But that didn't stop her from yelling. Or trying to.

Finally a roughneck looked up at them, waved back, and disappeared for a moment. When he returned he brought three of four other men he'd recruited and huddled with them long enough for a plan to emerge. Then they tied their heavy parkas together to make a net of sorts. They stretched it out as tight as they could get it and one of them called up for one of the girls to jump, making sure to land on their bottom if they could.

Pearl didn't think the oddly assembled mass of jackets looked to be anywhere nearly sturdy enough to put much hope in, especially from the top of a two-story building. But she didn't see any other options at the moment. So she stepped to the edge and took what amounted to a leap of faith, whether it be in God or parkas.

In a moment she was standing safely beside the men. Dorothy, who had followed Pearl's lead all afternoon, decided she might as well do it one more time and, in another moment, she was following her once again to find their parents.

≈

In Dallas Walter Cronkite reread the message he'd just torn off the UPI teletype machine. It was short, to the point, and sufficiently ominous to make him read it through three times.

Oil field sources report an explosion in the consolidated school in New London and request all available ambulances.

He took the copy into his bureau manager's office and was told to get his hat and coat.

And a car.

Twenty-Four

S eventy miles southeast of New London in Lufkin, twelve-year-old Al Vinson was on his bicycle delivering newspapers when he skidded to a stop and watched a line of military ambulances making their way quickly up South First Street, which was what the stretch of State Highway 59 was called that traveled though the city.

It wasn't uncommon to see convoys made up of jeeps, trucks, staff cars, and ambulances—all painted olive drab, the sad official hue of the Army— roll through Lufkin in early summer on the way down to the Gulf Coast town of Palacios for maneuvers. But it wasn't even officially spring yet. And this no-nonsense procession was nothing like those others, when townspeople were notified by the paper and the radio and came out to wave at the soldiers.

This convoy was fairly zipping along. And in the opposite direction of the summer pilgrimages.

One more thing young Al Vinson noticed as he peddled off to finish his paper route was that more than a few funeral home hearses were interspersed with the ambulances.

—

The digging went on by hand all afternoon.

The injured were either tended to by doctors and nurses who had come from nearby towns or were transported to hospitals in the area in ambulances or other vehicles.

The bodies of the dead were laid out along a fence at the edge of the school property, all of them covered by what must have looked like every sheet pulled from every bed in New London. Then, one by one, the bodies were carried out to the highway to whatever hearses had arrived or laid in cars or pickups. Some of the bodies were put in bread trucks, supplied by an area baker, to make the journey to funeral homes and makeshift morgues, the largest of which was in the American Legion hall in Overton.

Some parents lifted up their own children and took them to funeral homes in their own vehicles.

A few roughnecks who'd moved their families to New London for just the duration of the oil boom drove much further than to Henderson, Kilgore, Jacksonville, or Tyler while their wives cradled their broken, dead sons or daughters close to them.

A few drove very far indeed—hundreds of miles in some cases, well into the night—to take their children home.

≈

Radio stations in east Texas had discontinued their regular programming within an hour of the explosion and now devoted all of their airtime to the updates from New London.

The handsome new RCA Victor receiver in the office at Mother Francis Hospital in Tyler was tuned to the local station, its constant chatter serving as a backdrop to the frantic activity there. The telephone rang constantly, and one telegram after another arrived. Some of them were the last of the congratulatory notes and best wishes flowing in from other hospitals and Catholic communities, but most were offers of assistance from officials who assumed the new facility would be put to use very soon.

One telegram was from a Dr. Joseph Steele of Pittsburg, Pennsylvania, who was willing to travel to Texas along with some of his nurses. Another came from the administrator of Methodist Hospital in Dallas, who offered the services of his institution in any way needed. Other offers came, but Mothers Mary Ambrose and Regina chose to put off accepting any until they could get a clearer sense of the scope of the tragedy and the role, if any, that their hospital might play.

They didn't have to wait long.

Mother Regina, who as Superior Provincial of the Sisters of the Holy Family of Nazareth was the equivalent of an ecclesiastical field commander, had been awakened from her very short nap earlier in the afternoon and had dispatched ten nurses to New London. She looked at a wall clock and asked whoever was standing closest to her how far away the town was.

Twenty five or thirty miles, she was told. She looked at the clock again and made her calculation. The nurses should be just about getting there.

What Mother Regina didn't know was that on the way to New London the cars carrying the nurses had met a convoy of speeding ambulances with lights flashing and sirens blaring.

Before she and Mother Krueger had time to read through the messages offering help, the several ambulances skidded to a stop on the drive outside.

Then the two nuns opened the big doors to their new hospital and watched as attendants wheeled in twenty-four badly injured children.

Twenty-Five

By late afternoon Governor Allred had been told the size of the multitude that had arrived at the disaster site easily exceeded a thousand, perhaps much more than that, and hundreds of vehicles lined the roads in town and for miles out into the countryside in every direction.

State and county policemen and Texas Rangers were doing the best they could to keep onlookers out of the way and the roads open, but the general chaos hadn't subsided. And as news of the tragedy spread—by telephone, radio, afternoon editions of newspapers, and word of mouth—things weren't likely to get any better.

Put very simply, the governor was made to understand that there were just too many people there. He also suspected that confusion would naturally arise from the inevitable turf war between various law enforcement agencies tromping around in the same place. Too many chiefs and not enough Indians, the governor knew, wouldn't help matters a bit.

Then he might have reminded himself that he was the biggest chief of all, and that it fell entirely in his purview to call out the troops and declare martial law.

Now that, he must have figured, would slam the door on any number of problems and any amount of confusion and disorder.

In New London, the growing hoard of people watched as heavy equipment began arriving from the oilfields and timber tracts. Some of the larger contraptions came on long flatbed trucks that positioned themselves as close as possible; others, such as bulldozers and front-end loaders and tractors, harrumphed their way into town under their own power. Men scrambled to offload acetylene torches, winches, and hydraulic jacks from the backs of trucks.

The parents of children still unaccounted for watched the army of machinery being moved into place and knew that things had changed now. Now the rescue efforts were officially beyond what could be accomplished by strong backs and bloody hands. Now more muscle and horsepower was needed. More leverage.

And now, the parents realized, there would be more of a chance that the efforts to save their children might actually cause them more injury.

Or worse.

Twenty-Six

Shortly before nightfall several dozen big floodlights were brought in from the various oil companies' headquarters and set up, for nobody expected the work to stop until everyone who had been in the building at 3:17 had been found; be they alive or dead.

And that wouldn't be accomplished, everyone suspected, until this night had come and gone.

So now the positioning of the big lights just added to the general mayhem. Tractors and bulldozers growled and belched out black smoke, hundreds of roughnecks and policemen dug down into newly exposed pockets in the debris looking for survivors or bodies, rubble was still being ferried in peach baskets and by hand out to the campus perimeter, and way too many people—many of them parents waiting for news, others merely gawkers—were milling around.

Reporters from area radio stations and newspapers had shown up early on, and now more, from bigger places further away, were arriving in a steady stream. The local fellows had pitched in and helped dig at first. But with the influx of so many people they, like their quickly arriving brethren, had begun taking pictures and asking questions.

Details were sketchy, at best. The hastily printed extra editions of afternoon papers carried enormously large headlines followed by usually completely erroneous information. The first extra edition of the *Paris*—Texas, not France—*Evening News* proclaimed, in three-inch bold type, BLAST IN SCHOOL KILLS 500 IN NEW LONDON. This total nearly doubled what would actually be the correct number. An hour later, the second extra of the Evening News kept the three-inch letters but revised the death toll to six hundred and seventy.

Low clouds moved slowly in at the end of an afternoon in which there had been no clouds at all. The shadows they spread on the frantic goings-on made twilight darker than it was on most days.

Huge light bulbs attached to reporters' cameras exploded in brilliant bursts as dusk fell. Then the oil company's floodlights were turned on one by one. Finally the lights on the tall towers in the football stadium popped and sizzled and powered up.

It was in this surreal mixture of waning daylight, glaringly bright artificial illumination, deafening machinery, and more people than he'd ever seen in one place that Dalton Abercrombie, still in his bloody clothing, finally found his mother Virgie, sitting on the ground with two-year-old Talmage asleep in her lap.

She just couldn't stand up any longer, she told Dalton as she cried and hugged him close to her and tried to brush away the concrete particles that were lodged in his face and neck. The casts on Talmage's legs had seemed to get heavier and heavier, she told him, and she'd had to sit down. Just for a minute.

Then Virgie's husband Eric was there too, walking out of the throng of people almost like magic. He told them he'd been searching and searching for them, and Virgie could see the relief in his eyes.

But something else was there too.

Then Eric told them, having to work the few words carefully past the lump in his throat, that Boyd was dead.

What he didn't tell them was that he had just been shown the mangled body. Neither did he tell them that someone had said that Boyd — cheerful, constantly jabbering Boyd, singing as often as talking, smiling always — had been thrown a great distance, and had called out for his mother just before he died.

Virgie Abercrombie wasn't the only mother not told things that afternoon.

Twenty-Seven

In Wright City, Marvin Dee's supper had been kept warm for so long in the oven that the edges of the chicken and dumplings were beginning to crisp.

He should have already been home for a couple of hours, but Floy knew that things happened on the leases that sometimes required the men to work late. This wasn't an altogether bad thing, since some overtime pay would show up in the next paycheck.

But he'd never been this late.

Floy sat down on the first step of the front porch, hugged her knees, and watched day slowly surrender to night. What had only a few minutes before been splotchy shadows had expanded into a uniform darkness, making the road that she wished Marvin would walk down all but invisible.

She was searching through breaks in the slow moving clouds for the first star when the beams from a set of headlights bounced toward her. By the time the sedan had come to a stop and the driver leaned through his open window she was standing close enough to make out the logo of the Texas Company in the dim glow of the flare on the nearest derrick.

She listened carefully as he repeated the message he'd given to several wives already, then she asked how long it was likely to be before Marvin would come home. The company man just shook his head and said not to-night for sure.

When he was gone she went into the house and turned on the radio to listen to the reports from New London. Then she put the supper and pie into the ice box and grabbed up the car's keys and looked at them before putting them down again. The man on the radio had said there was already more than a thousand people there and Floy knew it would be difficult, if not impossible, to find one man in all of that. And not a very big man at that. Besides, she'd just be in the way.

At least she knew where he was. And she was confident that he would be okay; he had more common sense than most people she knew and he was cautious when doing a thing that might be dangerous.

So she wasn't worried about him being safe.

She was worried about what he was having to do. And see.

He was only twenty-one, like her. And she wasn't sure if he had ever even seen a dead person, other than maybe one or two laid out in coffins with their heads on satin pillows.

Now he was having to deal with more dead bodies in one day than most people would in a lifetime. In ten lifetimes.

She poured herself a glass of milk and considered making a sandwich. Then she sat down at the kitchen table with just the milk.

The news was fresh enough for her to be unable to keep the glass from shaking in her hand so she sat it down on the table and put her hands in her lap. She felt guilty that her first thoughts had been of Marvin and not of all of those poor children. Or for what their parents were going through.

She and Marvin wanted children but didn't have any yet. And even if they'd had one or two by now they wouldn't be old enough to have been at the school.

She tried to think of how it must feel to know that your child might be under that fallen building and need help. Or to wonder if they were already dead.

Then she thought again of Marvin, just a couple of years older than some of those students, searching for them.

She turned off the radio and sat at the table in the dark kitchen and listened to the thumping of the three oil wells nearby. In a little while she'd lay down.

But she knew she wouldn't sleep.

Twenty-Eight

T he rain started not long after dark.
There was no thunder or lightening to announce it, nor any wind whatsoever. The first drops weren't much more than a spitting business, as if Mother Nature was still deciding whether or not to make the effort at all. Then it started coming down with more purpose, and by the time everyone knew that it had settled in for the night the cakey dust that had swirled around and made a nuisance of itself all afternoon lay down like an exhausted pup and the ground turned slowly into mud.

People who lived close by went home and came back with blankets and raincoats. Umbrellas sprouted up in the crowd like so many mushrooms as onlookers kept their quiet vigil while the search continued for bodies. With the exception of a few survivors who might still be buried under debris, all of the injured had by now been tended to onsite and either sent home with their parents or transported to hospitals.

Now the mission had shifted from search and rescue to the removal of bodies, some of which were buried so deeply under heavy sections of the building that it would still be several hours before they were all found.

The ruined parts of the three rear extensions of the building loomed like bombed fortresses over the frantic activity of the workers, the mass of onlookers, and the growing group of new arrivals.

One of the new arrivals was Walter Cronkite, who'd just arrived from Dallas with his UPI bureau chief.

The cub reporter hadn't known what to expect during the several hour drive; there was no radio in the car, so all he and his companion had to go on was the brief initial report that had come over the wire that Cronkite was assigned to.

The chief had stopped at his favorite bootlegger's to refill his pocket flask on the outskirts of the city, then they'd watched the low clouds roll in as the sun set behind them. They didn't get any real insight into the magnitude of the story they were rushing to cover until they passed a funeral home in downtown Tyler and watched men unloading bodies from hearses, ambulances, and pickups parked as close to the establishment as they could get.

For the remaining twenty-five miles of their journey they drove straight for the abundance of bright light from the flood lamps and the stadium, like pilots locked in on a radio signal.

In New London, the chief figured out quickly that he wouldn't be able to find a parking place within at least a couple of miles of the school, so he drove until a state trooper waved him to a stop and he told Cronkite to hop out and get to work.

As he put the car in reverse, he rolled down the window and called out that they'd find each other later, but to go ahead and try to locate a telephone or a telegraph office so they could file a report. When Cronkite leaned in out of the rain and asked where he should look for a telephone the chief asked him how the hell he should know. He slammed the car into reverse and called out over the whirring engine that he'd been in this metropolis exactly as long as he had.

Cronkite, lean to the point of being skinny and in his early twenties, had no trouble sprinting the several hundred yards through mud and rain to where the lights were the brightest and the activity the most frantic. The only description he would ever be able to come up with for what he found there was that the countless workers were moving up and down the mounds of debris like a gigantic swarm of ants.

He would go on in his long career to describe battlefields, race riots, moon landings, and assassinations. He would go on to become everybody's Uncle Walter: the kind, wise, pillar of calm in any conceivable storm who would hold his loyal audiences' hands through many a dark night.

But on this night—a rainy March night in a tiny east Texas town in 1937— he was a gangly young fellow barely out of his teens who hadn't seen much of the world at all.

And nothing in the part that he had seen even came close to preparing him for the horror that lay before him, which very nearly took his breath away.

Twenty-Nine

In Tyler, the Bishop of the Catholic diocese of Dallas arrived at Mother Francis Hospital, which he was scheduled to formally open and consecrate the following afternoon, to find that it was already open and doing a brisk business.

The new state-of-the-art operating room was kept in constant use, and the beds were filling up in the wards. Doctors and nurses worked through the night as more ambulances arrived.

Mothers Krueger and Regina and the sisters in their charge worked through the night as well, seeing to the needs of doctors, nurses, and families who arrived with their children.

The ornate chapel, complete with what many of the parents might ordinarily associate with the bells and smells that were part and parcel of popery—statues, candles, and the stations of the cross—became, on this night, a place of prayer and meditation for a good many Baptists and Methodists.

It was going on six hours since the explosion, and still no one had any idea who was in charge of what. The police—state, local, and a group of tall Texas Rangers that moved around the crowd like long-legged cranes uncomfortable among shorter birds—had arrived in greater numbers all afternoon and evening, prompting one observer to say that it would be a perfect night to break the speed limit or rob a chicken coop, since every copper for hundreds of miles around seemed to have congregated in one place.

Officials from one agency or another continued to show up, some of them arriving on a small plane that landed at an airstrip near Henderson. President Roosevelt's medical advisor—at least one of them, since it's unclear how many he had or if they worked directly for him or the Surgeon General—showed up too, having driven over from Louisiana. Doctors and nurses were still coming in by the carload from as far away as Dallas and Houston, many of them volunteering for duty on the grounds, others going to area hospitals and doctor's offices to help there.

So now in addition to the hundreds of men still digging for bodies, lawmen, and the thousands of onlookers there were representatives of various official outfits, all of whom probably thought they were in charge.

Finally, Governor Allred made three announcements from Austin. First, a military board of inquiry would be appointed as soon as possible to determine the cause of the explosion. Second, all radio stations broadcasting in East Texas should inform their listeners that everyone with no business in New London should not go there. "I am pleading with the public not to go," his statement read, "and they will be turned back if they do."

The third gubernatorial decree was the one most people expected: that the school campus and an area of five miles surrounding it would be under martial law as of 8:00 p.m. This meant that after that time every decision would be made, until further notice, by a single military officer in charge of armed troops, and all law enforcement entities would be under his command.

Within an hour, units of the National Guard from several East Texas armories began arriving in convoys of olive drab trucks. Soldiers outfitted in full field gear and helmets climbed down quickly, armed with 1903 Springfield bolt action thirty aught six rifles and 45 caliber service automatic sidearms.

They fell into formations of platoons and companies, were called to attention by their commanders, and the night, already somber enough, took on a decidedly more ominous tone.

Thirty

T he shoulders upon whom all authority fell once martial law was declared belonged to one Lieutenant Colonel Clarence E. Parker, Regimental Commander of the 112th Cavalry, stationed in Tyler.

When his orders came through at 8:30 he'd already been in New London for over three hours, having driven over with some fellow American Legionaries to offer assistance. Now with his crown, as it were, firmly in place he assembled the commanders of all military troops—something like two hundred in all, from armories in Tyler, Longview, and Marshall—and the heads of the various law enforcement agencies and told them their most important duties were to see that the wrecking and rescue crews weren't hindered by the growing crowds and that personal property of citizens was protected.

Then he issued written orders that the immediate area, meaning the school campus, be cleared of all unnecessary people and vehicles ASAP and that entry posts be established and guards posted who would allow in only ambulances, doctors, nurses, wrecking and rescue crews, peace officers, reporters and photographers (as long as they behaved themselves) and school district personnel and parents there for the purpose of identifying the dead. All bodies were to be cleared though the military hospital and morgue before transport in ambulances or other vehicles. He also decreed that "all persons found carrying or picking up articles or property or pilfering are to be arrested and brought to military headquarters." Then he made mention of riot control. This in spite of the fact that the large crowd standing quietly in the rain, many praying and some crying, didn't seem particularly disposed to riot.

Several small skirmishes had broken out when some of the parents of injured or dead children had objected to reporters taking photographs. Everybody was at their breaking point now, or had long since passed it, and a few people didn't want any photos taken at all, even when there were no corpses or injured children anywhere around. One photographer from the Houston Post was pushed by an angry parent and his big camera thrown to the ground.

Enough time had elapsed since the explosion for rumors to take root. First, that somebody had blown up the school. Communists, most likely. Or an anarchist; there were, after all, stories about anarchists on the radio and newsreels all the time. Someone said he'd heard that a lunatic had escaped from the state asylum over in Rusk.

Finally somebody remembered that Mr. Shaw, the superintendent, had encouraged the school board, just a couple of months ago, to cut off service from the gas company and give him permission to have one of his janitors tap into the bleed off line from one of the oil leases.

This fresh morsel of information—which every New Londoner already knew to be a fact—spread quickly, and the use of the free gas became the culprit. The instability of the unrefined gas was made much of. And why a school with as much money as this one would cut such a corner and use green gas seemed suddenly odd, or downright irresponsible, to many in the crowd.

The crowd that was almost entirely made up, of course, of people who used the bleed-off gas in their own homes.

Walter Cronkite picked up on the general mumbling and asked someone where Mr. Shaw was. He was directed to the thin, exhausted gentleman with the bandage around his head who still wandered aimlessly through the ruins.

The superintendent—disoriented, completely devastated, and having learned earlier that his son Sam and two of his nephews had died in the explosion—answered the young reporter's direct question just as directly.

By midnight the crowd had dismissed all other theories, and there was no more talk of lunatics or anarchists or communists.

From then on, several armed Texas Rangers stayed close to Mr. Shaw.

Thirty-One

In the American Legion hall in Overton, parents moved quietly among bodies that had been laid out under sheets. One by one, their corners were slowly lifted up as parents tottered between hope and fear.

Sometimes the identification was easily made; in a few cases the faces were completely unmarked, as if they were only sleeping. Sadly, the process was usually more difficult.

One boy was so badly butchered that the only way his mother knew it was him was by the pocketknife he always carried. Other parents had to rely on hair ribbons, shoes, belts, and other items for clues to help identify their own children.

George Grigg lifted up sheet after sheet looking for his sons Horace and Edwin. But it was his boy William who spotted a bare foot sticking out from under a sheet across the room. It was missing the big toe. He pulled on his father's sleeve and they both knew that it was Horace, who had lost his toe the year before while playing with a pump jack.

They continued looking for Edwin, but when they were certain he wasn't there they carried Horace's body to their car and drove to a funeral home, stopping on the way to give his mother the sad news.

There was still hope, George told her, for finding Edwin alive.

Hope got mentioned pretty often in the families whose children hadn't been accounted for.

In those houses hope was the coin of the realm as midnight fell.

≈

The crowd had grown to perhaps more than two thousand people now, all of them standing in the slow, steady rain and watching men and machinery do their work. The abundance of brilliant illumination froze everything in a sprawling tableau of constantly mingling light and shadows.

Somewhere in the multitude of onlookers a woman started singing the opening verse of "Rock of Ages." Then someone else joined in, then one or two more. The crowd as a whole didn't take it up in earnest, and it was no match for the coughing, bellowing machinery anyway. Finally it died away completely.

The brightness of all the big lights rose up into the dark, rainy night and could be seen for miles around. Ten miles away, in Henderson, a little girl watched it from her yard and would always remember how brilliant and strong the light was, shooting straight up like that through the thick, low clouds.

It must, she would tell her great-grandchildren many years later, have been something like the light provided by the star over Bethlehem.

Photographs

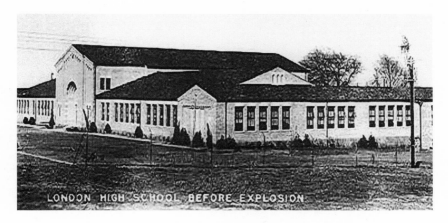

London High School before the explosion. Courtesy London Museum.

Mother Frances Hospital, Tyler, 1937. Courtesy London Museum.

Marvin and Floy Dees in 1937. Courtesy Marvin Dees.

The London softball team taken the day of the explosion. Ardyth Davidson is lower right.
Courtesy John Davidson.

Ardyth Davidson. Courtesy John Davidson.

Mr. Shaw being escorted away from the disaster. Courtesy London Museum.

Searching for survivors and bodies. Peach baskets were used to transport debris.
Courtesy London Museum.

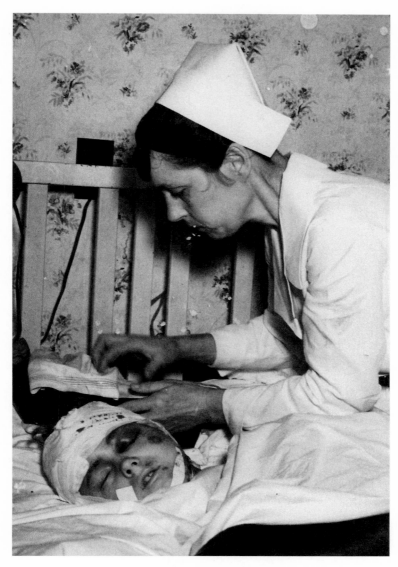

A nurse tending to an injured child. Courtesy London Museum.

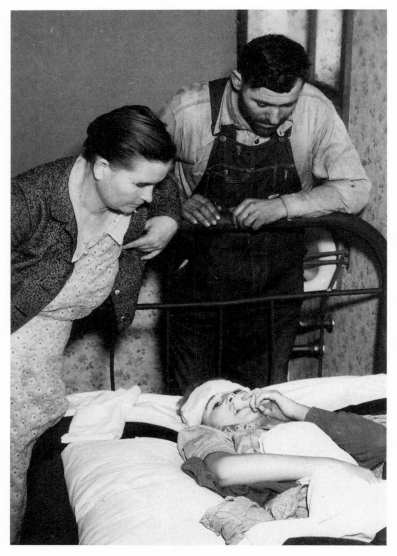

Parents with their injured child. Courtesy London Museum.

A "tapped" gas line. Courtesy London Museum.

Martial law. Courtesy London Museum.

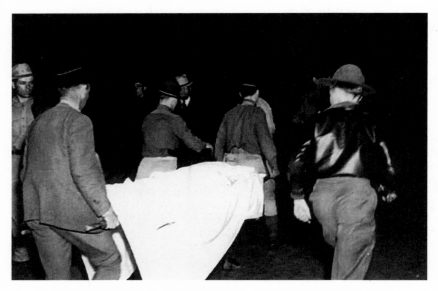

A body being removed from the debris field. Courtesy London Museum.

The Military Board of Inquiry. Courtesy London Museum.

A final farewell at Pleasant Hill Cemetery. Courtesy London Museum.

Marvin Dees today. Courtesy Ron Rozelle.

Part Three

The Long Silence

Thirty-Two

S ometime during the long night Thursday became Friday.

It rained continuously, softly at times and harder at others, but steady enough to make a mess of things. The rain fell straight down in the windless night through the beams of the big lights and splashed into puddles and onto the jagged rubble.

The crowd, standing close together in blankets and rain slickers under a spattering of open umbrellas, hadn't been diminished by either the rain or the lateness of the hour. If anything, it had grown since midnight. National Guard troops kept the onlookers back now, even the parents of children not yet accounted for, so the men and the machines had more room to move around in.

Marvin Dees was bone tired. He wasn't a big man, or a tall one. But he was lean and strong and could do a hard day's work and still have a spring in his step every afternoon when he walked home from the pipe yard.

If anyone had told him, before this night, that he could be so exhausted that chewing a bite of a ham and cheese sandwich would require a real effort he'd have called them crazy.

One of the foremen from the Texas Company had made it his business to find all the men and tell them their wives had been informed about where they were. Still, Marvin thought of Floy in their little house in Wright City. She'd be in bed now, though more than likely wide awake and thinking about him. And about all of this, he thought, as he looked around at the big, brightly lit area that was still a mighty busy place. All of the sheet-covered bodies that had been lined up along the far fence had been taken other places, he didn't know where, and newly discovered bodies were hurried off in the many ambulances that had returned from their several runs.

If asked how he felt then—after working a full day on the oil lease then spending nearly ten hours moving heavy debris and digging out bodies and helping to carry them, sometimes in pieces, out to the edge of the campus— he would have said he was tired, of course, but something more than that, too.

Shocked, maybe. Though that wouldn't be a good enough word. He was . . . dazed. Like something or someone that had been cold-cocked with a two-by-four but was still standing. He was just putting one foot in front of the other now, moving things and lifting up what was under them and carrying them away by rote.

He made sure not to look down at them anymore. For that had been al-most harder than he could handle at first. Now he willed himself to not think of them as people, or things that used to be people, but only as things. Like bricks and ceiling tiles and parts of walls were things.

He finished his coffee and sandwich and thanked the lady in the Salvation Army uniform who had provided them. Then he walked back to where he had been digging and thought again about Floy, alone in bed in the middle of the night in their warm, dry house.

At that moment Marvin Dees wanted nothing more out of life than to be there with her, with the rain falling outside their bedroom window and the whole bigger world, that included places like this one he was trudging through, on the other side of their locked doors.

Thirty-Three

Toward daylight, when there was increasingly less to be done and more men than were needed to do it, some of them sat on the running boards of cars and pickups and smoked and passed around pints of bourbon or rye, or mason jars of white lightning supplied by a local moonshiner. Because they were spent and brain weary, they needed a little fortitude—a bit of the old liquid variety Dutch Courage—to face the last of it.

By sunrise almost all of the bodies had been removed, all of the injured were in area hospitals or in larger ones in Houston or Dallas, or had been sent home with their parents. The regional director of the American Red Cross arrived somewhere around 4:00 a.m. and instructed his people to put together a list of those who were injured but had not gone to hospitals so they could be provided treatment if needed. They wanted to make sure everyone who had survived the explosion was being cared for.

The dead, who outnumbered the living, presented a bigger problem. The identification of the large number of unclaimed bodies was proving to be a long and tedious process.

Fingerprint experts had arrived in the wee hours of the morning and began taking prints of those children who had been so horribly disfigured that they weren't recognizable.

More than three hundred people from the New London area, many of them school children, had attended the Texas Centennial Exposition in Dallas the previous summer and, as a lark, had their fingerprints made at a law enforcement exhibit that was one of the most popular attractions. So a relatively substantial database of prints, quite rare at the time, did exist.

One of the fingerprint experts was quoted in the morning editions of newspapers that three hundred corpses were lying in improvised morgues in the Overton district alone. This was a number that would later prove to be too high, but there were, early Friday morning, many, many parents still searching for their children.

They usually started in the American Legion hall in Overton, since it was the largest of the makeshift morgues. Then if their child wasn't there they drove, or were driven by family or friends, from town to town and walked through hospitals, doctor's offices, funeral homes, gymnasiums, or wherever the living and the dead had been taken, all the while praying that their son or daughter would be finally discovered in a hospital bed.

Some prayers were answered in short order. William Grigg and his parents located Edwin, under heavy sedation with a punctured lung and back injuries that would keep him in the hospital for weeks. He wouldn't be told about his brother Horace's death until after the funeral, when his condition was stabilized.

Other families had to wait considerably longer for whatever verdict fate handed down.

The Shoemates made the circuit, much traveled that night, of East Texas towns looking for Sammie, the middle child. The scratches and cuts her older sister Doris had received when she'd been blown away from the building had been cleaned, daubed with mercurochrome, and bandaged early on. Then she'd spent the rest of Thursday afternoon wandering among the thousands of people who had congregated where the school used to be, looking for any Shoemate she could locate.

Her frantic parents found her shortly after dark. They'd known their youngest child, Elbert, was safe; they'd driven home to see if any of their brood had shown up and found his scribbled note that he had walked to his uncle's place. But their two girls were missing, and watching for hours as bodies were removed from the debris and carried out to the edge of the school property did nothing to bolster their confidence that they'd find them safe and sound.

Mrs. Shoemate had had a particularly hard time of it. She and Doris had argued early that morning, and the possibility that their last interaction would be a contentious one was almost more than she could tolerate.

So her reunion with her oldest child was a spirited explosion of hugs, kisses, and tears. With Doris, scraped and bruised, wincing through it all.

But what of Sammie? Who loved to sew and cook and crochet, things that interested her sister Doris not in the least, and who had small feet, cold as ice, that Doris had to contend with in the bed they shared.

During their traveling vigil her mother would turn occasionally and smile at her from the front seat. It was a feigned smile, however, a difficult mixture of joy at finding one daughter and dread of finding . . . whatever they might find.

They held each others' hand a good bit of the time, and every now and then Doris would reach up and rest her hand on the shoulder of her father, who grasped the wide steering wheel and looked stoically into the rainy night.

It wouldn't be until Saturday morning, nearly two full days after the explosion, that he would be shown the pitiful remains of a little girl in what had been a brown print dress with a square white collar. The stainless steel ring on one of the small fingers, made by an uncle who was a welder, shone brightly under the ceiling lights.

Several minutes later Mr. Shoemate would stumble out of the funeral home in Henderson supported by two other men. The look on his face would be all Doris and her mother needed to see, from inside the parked car, to know their journey had finally come to an end.

Thirty-Four

The Friday morning editions of perhaps every paper in the nation, and many others throughout the world, carried news of the New London tragedy.

In Texas, southern Oklahoma, Arkansas, and Louisiana the dailies were filled with multiple stories, sometimes filling whole sections, about the disaster. Some had run as many as three extra editions on Thursday and would run that many again on Friday.

The big papers—the *Dallas Morning News* and *Times Herald*, the *Houston Post* and *Chronicle*, the *New Orleans Times Picayune*, and others from San Antonio and Austin—dispatched reporters and photographers when the editors first learned of the explosion. So had the major wire services.

Walter Cronkite filed his first report within an hour of his arrival on Thursday night, from a telephone he had to beg for in an oil company field office. He and his chief were joined Friday morning by Delos Smith and Tom Reynolds, the senior United Press journalists at the time, who flew down from New York. Their most popular sports writer, Henry McLemore, was brought in from covering baseball spring training camps in Florida to write feature stories.

Cronkite would work straight through for over forty-eight hours, not falling into a bed in the Overton Hotel until Sunday morning. Of all the interviews he conducted—with families, survivors of the blast, townspeople, police officers, and federal officials—almost certainly the most important, and personally painful, was with Mr. Shaw, who had wept as he told him he'd asked the school board for permission to tap into the free gas.

By midmorning most papers were reporting that the situation in New London was now under control.

One headline, representative of many others similar to it, screamed out in towering letters, "Laborers Cease Digging After 425 Bodies Recovered from School Ruins" then, just a bit smaller, "'Job is Finished' They Aver, 'Every

Brick is Turned.'" The body count fluctuated widely from publication to publication, and even from morning to evening editions of the same paper.

The Associated Press circulated a piece about a thirty-eight-year-old oilfield worker in Bellville, Texas, two hundred miles southwest of New London, who, though having no connection with either family or acquaintances
there, was apparently so distraught by radio reports of the disaster that when
his brother tried to settle him down, he threatened to kill him. He then loaded
both barrels of a shotgun as proof that he was prepared to suit the action to
the word. The brother called a county deputy sheriff, who came to the scene
and was threatened as well. The deputy promptly shot and killed the man,
and was immediately forgiven by the brother, who said the lawman had no
other choice.

In every publication the New London updates invariably ran close to and
oftentimes beside or beneath reports of aviator Amelia Earhart's attempt to
circumnavigate the globe. If successful, she wouldn't be the first to do it, but
her route, which basically followed the equator, would be the longest ever
attempted. She and her navigator Fred Noonan had taken off on Wednesday
and were now in Honolulu, Hawaii, pondering the next leg of the journey.
America, it seems, anxiously awaited their decision. Perhaps the only things
that could compete, news-wise, would have been a war or disaster. The explosion of a school did the trick, failing to knock Amelia off the front page, but
usually nudging her aside from the center for a day or two.

But not always.

The Ada, Oklahoma, *Evening News* had Earhart's adventures in its accus-
tomed place and buried several of the New London wire service reports on
page five, with a long litany of goings-on around town, such as "J. D. Spence
and daughter Madeline of Stonewall attended to business and shopped in Ada
on Friday," and a big advertisement for Martha Washington sliced bread—"a
glass of milk in every loaf. No foolin', it's *good!*" The paper also contained
Alley Oop's daily strip, and a piece titled "Constipation May Lead to Colds,"
which offered precious little in the way of scientific evidence, but accolades
galore for All Bran cereal, made and "guaranteed" by the Kellogg Company,
which undoubtedly bought the space on the condition that it be formatted as
hard news.

The headline writer at the *San Antonio Light,* obviously given to infusing
his or her creations with as much high drama as possible, came up with these
gems for Friday, which read like teasers for horror movies: "Torn Bodies in

Legion Hall," "Town Greets Dawn of Tragedy in Silence," "Hole in Wall Exit for Few," and "Coffin Makers Swamped."

In fact, coffin makers *were* swamped. Production had to be stepped up considerably to fill orders from East Texas undertakers. Casket manufacturers in Dallas reported the biggest demand in the city's history for medium-sized coffins, the model used almost exclusively for children.

Thirty-Five

Sixteen-year-old John Fuhr, one of only five survivors of Miss Lizzie Thompson's tenth grade English class of twenty-two, stepped in front of newsreel cameras at midmorning and recounted the events of the previous afternoon with the ease of a professional correspondent.

His brief comments would be watched by millions of people in movie theatres across the nation over the next few days. Sandwiched between the cartoon and the feature film, daily newsreels of current events were the precursors to what would one day be the evening news on television. The last few days of the middle week of March would have had something, surely, about hard times and President Roosevelt's New Deal programs—a galaxy of three- and four-letter acronyms that citizens were finally starting to make some sense of —and certainly an update on Amelia Earhart's island-hopping odyssey. And there would be this lanky young fellow standing in the ruins of what had been, just the previous afternoon, his school.

His tall Nordic good looks might have misled audiences into thinking that the blonde lad must hail from somewhere like Minnesota or Oslo or Berlin. Until he opened his mouth, that is: a slow East Texas drawl ambled out like thick syrup oozing over the edge of a spoon.

He was wearing a Boy Scout uniform because his local troop leader had volunteered his scouts early that morning, and they were put to work helping with crowd control and running various errands. Oddly enough, they were armed with rifles. But someone very wise indeed had decided that they not be issued any bullets.

The New London segment of the newsreel began with the image that was the symbol of the Pathe News Agency, a crowing rooster, as recognizable to moviegoers as the MGM lion. After a fast-talking, unseen announcer gave a speedy account of the disaster over moving images of devastation and busy relief workers, up stepped John Fuhr, not wielding a rifle, to a flat disc microphone as wide as a saucer. He didn't stand ramrod straight, which would have broadcast nervousness or insecurity, but with his hands in his pockets and listing slightly to starboard. He identified himself, said he was in the tenth grade—"There were one hundred and seventy of us in that class," he said, managing to elongate "class" into two lengthy syllables—and said he'd been in Miss Lizzie Thompson's room learning about Mr. Edgar Allan Poe when something went boom, the wall fell away, Miss Thompson was killed, and he, uninjured, dragged two girls out. One had a bad gash in her head, the other one was already dead.

Sitting through his slow, carefully worded rendition after the rapid-fire delivery of the announcer must have been, for audiences, like hearing an engine being shifted down from its highest gear to its lowest.

Two other Boy Scouts, or perhaps young lawmen, stood behind John, one of them comfortably cradling the wooden stock of his rifle in the crook of one arm. People milled around a big piece of heavy equipment in the background, and the persistent cloud of dust wandered by, like someone who strolls before rolling cameras hoping to get in the shots.

John ended by saying he hadn't known what to do, and that bodies had been lying all over the place like kindling wood. He paused a moment, and finally said it looked like somebody had lifted the lid off a kettle.

Then footage of injured children in hospital beds filled the screen as the announcer assured viewers that the "pitifully small victims" were being aided by both the very best medical attention and the prayers of the nation.

"Four hundred others," he concluded, slowing down to make the most of his parting words, "would play, would laugh, would learn no more."

The number would prove to be much too high, of course. As newspaper, radio, and newsreel crews scurried around so soon after the event, any number would do.

The higher the better.

Thirty-Six

In Tyler, some of the injured children receiving the care the newsreel announcer spoke of were in Mother Francis Hospital.

Doctors who would be on staff once the brand new facility officially opened had worked through the night, along with other physicians who'd just shown up, some of them from miles away, to pitch in. Nurses, nuns, and volunteers had labored nonstop since the first children were brought in by ambulances the previous evening.

Mother Mary Ambrose, the hospital administrator—along with Mother Regina and Bishop Joseph Patrick Lynch of Dallas, both of whom had come to Tyler for the dedication of the building—had seen to the practical and spiritual needs of patients, family, and staff for so many hours that they were pretty much running on pure adrenaline now, as was everyone else in the white, four-story hospital on the hilltop. The only people getting any sleep were children in beds in the wards, some of them under sedation, others simply worn completely out from the ordeal.

Early that morning the bishop had invited anyone who could take a brief few moments from their duties to the chapel for an abbreviated mass. This was a legitimate invitation to the families of injured children, and something more compulsory for Roman Catholics.

There, minus the many guests to whom Mother Mary Ambrose had mailed engraved invitations, and without speeches and hymns and cake and punch, the bishop invoked the blessings of God on Mother Francis and on all who would work there. Then he consecrated the building and its service to His glory. He asked all the saints—and Saint Joseph specifically, it being his feast day—to pray for the hospital and for the children who died in the disaster, those who survived it, and their loved ones.

There is no record that Bishop Lynch alluded to the age old paradox surrounding the suffering of the innocent. This was probably just as well, since the good Catholics who had dealt with an abundance of such suffering in the last many hours and the parents, attending their first and probably only mass, were all then painfully aware that the Almighty does indeed move in mysterious ways.

≈

The world was taking note now, on the morning after the catastrophe.

The president of the Texas State Teacher's Association received messages of sympathy from both the Teachers Association of France and the International Federation of Teachers, which represented twenty -nine countries. In Austin, Governor Allred was deluged with telegrams expressing sympathy and offers of support from his counterparts in nearly every state. The mayor of New York City, Fiorello La Guardia, personally telephoned the mayor of Henderson, the nearest incorporated municipality to New London. The mayor of Henderson, not quite knowing how to respond to the offer of any manpower or medical supplies needed, thanked La Guardia profusely but assured him that aid was coming in from sources much closer at hand.

Shortly after noon on Capitol Hill in Washington the Senate and the House of Representatives paused to pay official attention to the tragedy. Whatever long-winded speeches or spirited debates were on tap for the afternoon sessions were delayed briefly so the respective chaplains could offer up prayers for the people of the small town that almost no one in the two chambers had ever heard of.

After the prayers, several condolences were offered from the floors and a few Texas members spoke some carefully chosen words into the Congressional record, after which federal aid was requested and promptly approved. Then, the right thing having been done, the members of the two chambers sat back in their seats and the business of democracy moved on.

Down Pennsylvania Avenue at the White House the office of the president—without him in it, since he was in Warm Springs, Georgia— received a cornucopia of official messages regarding the disaster from foreign embassies in Washington and from heads of state around the world.

Here was one:

On the occasion of the terrible explosion at New London, Texas, which took so many young lives, I want to assure your Excellency of my and the German peoples' sincere sympathy.

It was signed Adolf Hitler, German Reich Chancellor.

Thirty-Seven

By late morning on Friday the rain had finally moved on to pester some other place. A few straggling clouds stayed put, and sunlight slipped hesitantly through them now and then, as if reluctant to step in among such sad doings.

Things were winding down. Now it would be a matter of machines pushing down the remnants of the trio of two-story sections that had been the rear extensions of the E-shaped structure. Then that rubble and any other that had not already been moved would be loaded into dump trucks and taken away to be spilled into gullies and any low-lying places that could stand to be higher.

It would later be estimated by the Bureau of Mines that in a period of less than twenty-four hours a workforce of perhaps a thousand men—the lion's share of them having volunteered after a full day's work in the oil fields—moved approximately four million pounds (something like two thousand tons) of debris from the site, most of it by hand.

For the men who had been there from the beginning, the work was done. Fathers of children who had been in the building were either attending to their treatment and healing or making arrangements to bury them. Men who had no children were exhausted. Newer arrivals, fresher men who had slept a bit or had just arrived, still searched for bodies. But there were few, if any, to be found now.

So Marvin Dees went home.

The same crew truck that had brought him into town took him, over twenty hours later, out again. The men didn't talk as the truck climbed and descended low hills on the narrow ribbon of highway flanked by towering trees and sporadic oil derricks. Out here, Marvin thought, past Turnertown and past the parked cars and trucks and the hordes of people, it looked like it did every day, as if nothing had changed at all. He watched a red-tailed hawk fly high up in the midday sky.

Floy was standing on the porch when he got out of the truck. He didn't say anything to the other men or even so much as look at them, but kept his eyes on Floy as they drove away.

After a shower and a change of clothes he sat at his place at the kitchen table where he'd eaten breakfast an eternity ago. Before the day and night and half of another day had somehow transpired. Before the world shifted, and the whole sky turned around.

He looked at the plate of warmed-over chicken and dumplings and smiled, almost saying, as he always did, what perfect, thin dumplings she made. But the words weren't there just yet. She sat down, too, and smiled back at him.

He lifted up his fork and, after a moment, put it down again.

When he closed his eyes Floy reached over and held his hand in both of hers. They sat like that for a long while.

≈

By twilight almost nothing of the building that had been the junior high and high school remained. By the next morning everything would be gone.

True, the wide lawn that had been in front of the school would be trampled down, gouged out, and ruined. But spring would officially arrive in a few days and grass, being at least as persistent as the dust that still floated over the place, would find its way up slowly through the scars and cover everything over soon enough.

The seniors had studied a poem by Carl Sandburg about just that very thing in their English class a few days before. It was titled "Grass." "'Pile the bodies high at Austerlitz and Waterloo,'" their teacher had read aloud as bright sunlight streamed in through the tall windows in her classroom. "'Shovel them under and let me work. I am the grass; I cover all.'"

Her students had listened politely, probably happy that they'd not been required to memorize the poem. Some of them had probably been thinking of their graduation ceremony, which would take place in just a couple of months in the big auditorium down the hall. Or of the upcoming county meet in Henderson, the promise of a long weekend, or of Easter, just over a week away. Perhaps they had been thinking any number of things that sunshine and pleasant weather could inspire after the cold, gray months of bare, skeletal trees, heavy coats, and shut, frosted-over windows.

Almost all of the students in that room would be dead before any of those things would come to pass.

"'I am the grass,'" their teacher had read. "'Let me work.'"

Thirty-Eight

The funerals began on Saturday, even while the last of the rubble was being cleared away.

But the majority were conducted the next day. So many, in fact—several newspapers reported over two hundred on that Sunday alone—that churches in the area cancelled regular worship services, and local businesses posted schedules in their windows.

During that weekend, and again on the first days of the next week, the soft cadence of hymns—"What a Friend We Have in Jesus," "In the Garden," "Amazing Grace," and other standards, all so well-known and so often sung that few hymnals were opened—floated out of the open windows of churches in funeral after funeral as the surrounding towns sent their children off to God.

The Baptist church in Overton, a square, no-nonsense box of a building, was the setting for more services than any other. Hearses and pickup trucks, sometimes as many as a dozen or more at a time, sat in front of the church displaying caskets covered with floral lays as a forest of oil derricks rose up all around, the pumps beneath them thumping away in tune with the slow singing.

People went from one funeral to the next (very few were for only one child, and some were for a dozen or more at a time) like workers reporting for extra shifts. The women wore their best print dresses and—if they weren't overly festive—the hats they hadn't intended to take down from the closet shelf until a week later, for Easter. The men wore the one suit in their wardrobes designated official church and funeral garb with wide, short neckties; not the ones splashed with bright colors they wore to picture shows or dance halls, but the darker one. The funeral tie.

A common tradition in that time and place was to bring food to the homes of bereaved families. Family and friends could have a slice of pear or jam cake with their coffee when paying their respects, and platters of fried chicken, baked ham, deviled eggs, and a tureen of deep-dish chicken pie would fill a table for the crowd that always showed up after the service and the burial.

But there were just too many bereaved families all of a sudden for the tradition to be practical. One lady, whose apple pies were great favorites among funeral goers, made the comment that there just wasn't enough food in the garden, on trees, or in the grocery stores to feed everybody who had somebody to bury.

Area funeral homes had to hire extra workers to dig the graves, most of them in the Pleasant Hill cemetery a few miles up the Henderson highway, others in burying grounds in towns and scattered throughout the countryside. Somebody suggested that everyone who perished in the disaster be buried in what would become a memorial park, but the parents nixed that quickly, saying they wanted their children buried in existing cemeteries with family, some of whom were already there, others who would follow along in due course.

There was no way that providers of tombstones could keep up with the sudden demand for either the stones themselves or names, dates, and other inscriptions—"Weep not; she is at rest," "Our baby," "At play in the fields of the Lord"—that had to be chiseled into them. Tombstones would be delivered to cemeteries for weeks to come, sometimes having to be moved from grave to grave in the ensuing confusion.

Some businesses in New London and Overton put up lists of the missing and the dead in their windows, partly as a way of remembering and honoring the victims, but also as a practical matter. Names were crossed through as bodies were identified, each black line moving everything a bit closer to a conclusion.

By Sunday morning only one small body, a young girl, lay unclaimed in the American Legion hall in Overton.

Workers there were sure it had to be Wanda Emberling, whose father had made the rounds of all the places where bodies had been taken since Thursday afternoon.

When only one tiny, sheet-covered mound was left, he looked again at the remains that were too disfigured to be recognizable and maintained that it was not his daughter.

Word went out that anyone who might be able to identify the young victim should come and take a look. Oscar Worrell, who had helped with the identification of other bodies, had already stood over this one once before, thinking something about her seemed familiar.

His ten-year-old cousin, Dale May York, was the same height, with the same slight build, and looked to be about the same age as this girl. In fact, Dale May could be this girl, except for one problem.

She'd been buried the day before at the Pleasant Hill cemetery.

Still, he asked if he could see the left foot.

And there on the left big toe was the peculiar scar Dale May had been left with after she'd let a garden hoe slip in her hands while weeding.

Within an hour or so, the body of who had been believed to be Dale Mae was exhumed with her parents and the Emberlings attending. The remains of the girl in the reopened coffin were also mangled. But Mrs. Emberling, just as Dale May York's cousin had, asked to see the feet. Her daughter, Wanda, had colored her toenails with crayons on Wednesday night. One quick look convinced her mother that the mix up had been sorted out.

Dale May York and Wanda Emberling finally ended up buried not very far apart, under stones bearing their correct names.

If anyone thought it peculiar that such a mistake could have occured, they would have only to recall how many bodies had been sent to so many locations after being hurriedly identified and tagged at the site of the explosion.

Then they would have likely considered it surprising that it only happened once.

Thirty-Nine

The court of inquiry mandated by Governor Allred convened at nine o'clock on Saturday morning in the band hall of the school, one of the several outbuildings on campus that had been far enough removed from the main building to have suffered no damage more substantial than broken windows.

The assistant Adjutant General of Texas, Major Gaston Howard, was the president and presiding officer. The rest of the board was comprised of the director of the Texas Department of Public Safety, a couple of army captains — at least one of which was in the Judge Advocate's office — and Edward P. Clark, the Texas Secretary of State, who is listed in one official report as a first lieutenant and a later one as a captain. So either a mistake was made in the documentation or Mr. Clark was given a promotion during the course of the proceedings. This is unlikely, since the board heard its evidence, deliberated, and reached its conclusions in the span of just four days.

Also sitting in at the invitation of either the governor or Major Howard was a chemistry professor, Dr. Schoch, from the University of Texas who, as a recognized expert on explosives, had been sent by Governor Allred to New London with a Highway Patrol escort the day before. Also on the panel were the district attorney for Rusk County, who had the appropriately rustic and rural name of Stone Wells, and a member of the legislature, State Senator Joe Hill of Henderson.

Major Howard had relieved Colonel Parker, who now sat as a member of the tribunal, of his martial law responsibilities upon his arrival in New London sometime during the night. By then, the crowd had dwindled down substantially and the wrecking crews had all but finished their job, so most of the troops had been sent home. Martial law would officially remain in effect until the governor saw fit to lift it, but only a small contingent — one officer and twenty-seven men of Troop F of the 112th Calvary — remained on duty.

The opening statement by Major Howard was brief and very much to the point. He said that he and his fellow officers had not been charged to be a criminal court, but were only interested in determining the cause of the explosion and hopefully preventing it from ever happening again.

They worked quickly and efficiently through their business over the next few days, hearing testimony from over fifty people, everyone from the janitors of the school to its superintendent and board president, and from eyewitnesses to technical experts who'd been invited from universities and industry.

A good many cigarettes and pipes were smoked as the men leaned over tables and took their spectacles off and put them on again. Charts and blueprints and topographical maps were laid out and then rolled up. Photographers could snap pictures, the exploding flashes erupting sporadically during the proceedings, but reporters, though allowed to scribble notes, had to refrain from asking any questions while the court was in session. The huge gas regulator—a bulky, cast iron contraption, banged up a bit from the explosion—that had modified the pressure of all gas entering the school was laid out on one big table; the men came up and looked at it as they would at a fresh-killed whitetail buck in the back of somebody's pickup truck.

The first witness called, the architect of the school, testified that he had designed a building to be heated by steam generated in a boiler, which is what he had been asked to do. Therefore no extensive ventilation system had been included in the crawl space where the gas had collected. The few vents that were there, he said, were for temperature control and "wouldn't be worth a dime" for anything else. Next up was the contractor, who said the school had met the building code of the city of Henderson, the county seat, but again, for a boiler system for steam heating, not gas.

One fellow, who hadn't won the bid for the school's heating system, had fired off a letter to Governor Allred at the time and now found himself in the witness chair. He claimed to have warned the school officials about the danger of changing their original plans in favor of gas heaters and he told the court that he saw it as a crime to put those things in buildings.

He was, of course, in the business of selling boilers.

A representative of the Parade Gasoline Company, into whose bleed-off lines the school had tapped for free gas, testified that no one had been given permission to connect to that pipeline, which ran close by the school. The first he knew of it, he maintained, was after the explosion, when he sent a crew to disconnect the line.

This explanation, after a long moment of stunned silence, brought more than a few coughs and a subdued laugh or two.

Forty

One of the first witnesses called on Monday morning was the superintendent of the London Consolidated School District.

Mr. Shaw was dressed, to the surprise of absolutely no one who knew him, in a three-piece dark suit, the collar of his stiff dress shirt pinched tight against his thin neck, and a black tie. He wore his thick eyeglasses and, since he was inside, his fedora sat on the table beside his slender hands, which were clasped together.

He had aged considerably in the last few days. His seventeen-year-old son Sam, called Sambo, had been killed in the explosion, along with two of his nephews and a majority of the junior high and high school students in his school. And he hadn't been a young man even before all of that. He was pale and obviously tired. A fresh bandage was wrapped around one hand.

He answered the questions put to him in a clear voice, though with much less of the vigor with which he'd addressed school assemblies and faculty meetings. He paused from time to time, either choosing the next words very carefully, or losing his train of thought for a moment.

When he was asked if he had been given permission from the Parade Gasoline Company to have one of his janitors tap into the bleed off-gas line, everyone in the room stopped what they were writing and watched him.

The night before, the evening papers had run an interview with the vice president of the company in Shreveport who said that Earl Clover, the superintendent of the plant near New London, had refused to give permission when asked for the gas.

Mr. Shaw first seemed confused by the question, thought a moment, then said that he had spoken with Clover about it, and came away thinking that he hadn't objected to it.

Low whispers and the scratching of pens and pencils on pads moved through the room like a slow breeze through dry grass. Then Mr. Shaw sat straighter in his chair and make a point of the fact that Clover had not given him permission, "any definite permission at all."

He went on to say that the school board had not made the decision; that it had been his alone and all he'd gotten from the board was an okay to proceed. He'd even been warned, he said, by the United Gas Service, where the school had purchased natural gas until he hadn't renewed the contract, that there might be some danger in using the wet, or green, gas.

He said he thought they'd said that just because they wanted the business, which amounted to about two hundred and fifty dollars a month.

A bit later Mr. Shaw broke down and was given permission to go and rest. He wouldn't be called again.

When he was gone, E. W. Reagan, the president of the school board, was called. His testimony was brief.

When asked if he had had any dealing with the Parade Gasoline Company in regards to the current matter, he stated that he had nothing to do with it at all.

He said that Shaw said it would be all right.

The members of the court and every reporter in the room wrote it down, word for word.

Shaw said it would be all right.

Forty-One

The Court of Inquiry determined, after considering and deliberating all of the testimony they'd heard, that the cause of the disaster was—no surprise here—the explosion of a vast accumulation of odorless natural gas in an improperly ventilated crawl space beneath the London school.

Regarding the specific cause, one of the witnesses had been one of only two surviving students who had been in the manual training room and watched instructor Lemmie Butler flip the switch that threw the spark that ignited the gas.

As to how the gas got into the crawl space in the first place, no evidence— conclusive or otherwise —was offered. Dr. Schoch, the explosives expert, had run some tests and determined it hadn't seeped in through the ground, and the big regulator had been dismantled and found to be in no way defective.

So the culprit had to be a break in the pipe that ran around the entire outer wall of the enclosed area.

One story that had gotten a good bit of attention since the blast was about a group of boys (though it was never clear *which* boys) who'd been seen pushing down on a capped gas line that emerged from the concrete floor. They liked the way it felt when they stepped on it, and how it came back up again for more. One time, the storytellers always said, it didn't come back up at all.

The use of free gas from a bleed-off line was a *leitmotif* that ran through much of the testimony. One witness, J. C. Karens, a member of the school board, had remembered things a bit differently than Mr. Clover, the plant manager for the Parade Gas Company, and Mr. Reagan, the president of the board.

He testified that Clover *had* known of the connection to the residue line and had said that, while the company discouraged such use, he had no personal objection to it. Mr. Karens went on to indicate that the use of free gas from all of the various oil companies in the area was a very common procedure.

Which was an understatement if ever there was one.

≈

The proceedings were gaveled to a close on Tuesday, March 23, at about the same time the governor decreed that a state of martial law no longer existed. No arrests had been made nor any incident of disorderly conduct recorded during the several days of its enforcement.

True to Major Howard's word in his introductory statement, no blame was assigned. Neither would it be in another investigation by the United States Bureau of Mines published in December.

The military court of inquiry made several specific recommendations regarding the construction and ventilation of public buildings. But the two that would eventually bring about the most changes, and which would be put forth again several months later in the Bureau of Mines report, were that it be mandated as soon as possible that a warning agent with a distinctive odor be introduced into all natural gas and that anyone installing any fixtures or working with any connections on lines containing gas be trained and certified in that particular craft.

In neither report was it alluded to or stated that the use of free gas in the school had been the cause of the explosion. In fact, the Bureau of Mines stated unequivocally that the explosion would have occurred if the gas had been free or paid for. The properties of the two products would have made no difference.

At the simplest level, the facts were very, very simple indeed: The gas was odorless, so nobody knew it was there.

But it *was* there.

And it blew up.

≈

The fact that nobody was found guilty of anything didn't sit well with many parents of dead children who needed somebody to blame. Somebody more tangible than the government. Or fate. Or God.

A group of one hundred and seven parents and ninety other people who called themselves "concerned citizens" would send a petition to President Roosevelt, informing him they weren't satisfied with the findings of the military board and were requesting a more thorough investigation.

Which they wouldn't get. Unless, that is, they would choose to consider the upcoming Bureau of Mines proceedings to be the result of their demands, which it couldn't be since it had already been scheduled to convene, and would eventually reach the same conclusions and even more adamantly refuse to cast blame on any individuals.

Something like seventy lawsuits would be filed—against Mr. Shaw, the school board, or the Parade Gasoline Company—but only a few would actually come to trial. And those would be quickly dismissed due to lack of evidence.

Still, Mr. Shaw and his request to the school board to tap into the free gas fell under a cloud of suspicion that wasn't likely to lift any time soon, and was the subject of all manner of conjecture, from mumbled accusations to angry rants.

Perhaps he knew all along that he couldn't stay. And it might have been something of a relief when the board either dismissed him outright or asked him to resign. It wasn't clear which, but the end result was the same.

Their official response was that they appreciated his long, faithful service and, while no blame was being cast, it would be best for the community for there to be a change.

Being the man he was, he was gracious to the end. He replied publicly to the board's dismissal in a letter that was published in an area paper. He started by saying that he wasn't appealing for sympathy, then he had only nice things to say about the board he'd worked for and the teachers who'd worked for him. His highest praise was for all the students who'd attended the school. He concluded by thanking people throughout the nation for their "splendid spirit of helpfulness."

Never, at any time, did he say that the disaster hadn't been his fault.

He would move back to Minden, where he'd been the superintendent before coming to New London; he'd finish out his career there and then retire. Some would say a job was created for him there that didn't involve teaching children. Some would say he had a nervous breakdown. Others would be less kind, and say he cracked up completely.

Others would maintain he was just a good man who'd been made a scapegoat or, perhaps more tragically, had fallen on the sword because he saw it as his place, his duty, to do so.

Some New Londoners would go to their graves blaming him.

They had to blame somebody.

Forty-Two

On Monday, March 22, while the Board of Inquiry was still about its business and some of the dead were yet to be buried, a New London junior high student, Betty Jo Hardin, wrote a letter to a friend who had recently moved away.

The penciled text is in the tentative, looping cursive of a child who had obviously been put though her paces on lined tablets in penmanship class. The paper would age during the ensuing years, until it is finally a brittle, dusky brown, like a leaf pressed for decades in the pages of a book.

It's a hodgepodge of mechanical, punctuation, and spelling errors.

But the missive itself is perhaps as true and fine a testament of the several days the town had just lived through as any that survived or would come later.

Monday

Dear Jewel,

Hows school. I hope your getting along fine in school. I haven't even got any school to go to. I wish I could come and go to school with you but I guess I cant. Jewel I was in the explosion which you have already heard about. And of course you want to know how I got out well heres how. In our room we didn't even know it came till it hit us. It knocked me out for a minute and when I did come to every thing from bricks to plaster was on my head. I wiggled till I got my head off the desk and then fell down in to the isle waiting for more explosion. But when it didn't come I just had to take my time and take one brick off at a time. I had on a black dress and it was as white as snow and my hair and everybody elses that got out in my room looked like we had turned gray headed. I had to jump one story to the ground. I was in arithmetic and that is in Miss Gores room. Our room wasn't hurt much and thats the reason we all got out. The two walls caved in. Margie Strickland had just stepped out the door of the building when it came. She wasn't hurt.

I've been going to funerals day in and day out. I didn't look at Geneva because I wanted to remember her as she was. Well Jewel I guess all our friends such as Geneva, Rachel Mae, and Freddy have passed away and I can't express my feeling in a letter. Donald and I got togather. Mr. Waggner and Mr. Waldrip got out. Mr. Wagg had his hand on the door ready to go in when it happened. Miss Phyrus got out with her dress torn off of her. All I got was a black nose and teeth knocked loose and a chin that hurts as if it weere brocken. As I walked around to the front of the building after I got out I saw many of our friends laying among the stones and bricks with arm, head, and legs near their body. Thank God Jewel you were not in it. I guess it was just luck with me. The only ones left in the gang is Margie and I. You and Fay. Mr. Jolly is taking it mighty hard about Geneva. Geneva was takng her taking her piano lessons and was found near Miss Price after the explosion. Geniva lived a few minutes while being brought out on the stretcher but didn't say anything. Dorthy White was killed and Miss Bell, Miss Barns, Miss Gore, Miss Hanna, Miss Neal, and Miss Arnold. Im glad Im able to write the letter.

Your far away friend,
Betty Jo

P.S. I guess you think this letter is kinda cold but I'm nearly sick from thinking about it. A reporter at Henderson found my autograph book in the wreckage at the side and put it in the paper. I've felt bad so much about it I can't feel anything any more. You know how I feel.

Forty-Three

Exactly one week after the explosion Carolyn Jones, a New London fifth grader in a neatly pressed, puffy-sleeved blue cotton dress, stood on a chair behind an ornate rostrum and addressed a packed session of the Texas Senate in the state capitol building in Austin. The famous six flags that had flown over that fabled land rose up behind her, like the plumes of a gigantic peacock.

An hour later she was escorted down a wide corridor, through the massive rotunda, across the glistening lone star in the state seal inlaid in the marble floor beneath the towering dome—typical of Texan bluster, mere inches shorter than that of the national capitol in Washington—and along another massive hallway to the House of Representatives, where she gave the speech a second time.

Much would be made in the press about how confidently Carolyn appeared before the two assemblies, and of how seldom she looked down at her notes. When asked about it, she told reporters she'd been up till nearly midnight rehearsing.

Her most quoted sentence, which found its way into wire service reports and hundreds of afternoon editions of newspapers, was a masterpiece of emotion-tugging rhetoric: "Our daddies and mothers as well as our school teachers want to know that when we leave our homes in the morning to go to school we will come out safe when our lessons are over."

Then she asked that a memorial day be set aside and a fund established for the survivors and families of victims, with any money left over going to an endowment to help provide college educations for any surviving students who wanted one.

Carolyn might have written the words herself, but it's more likely they were the product of an early version of spin doctoring. Perhaps by Senator Joe Hill of Henderson, who had been instrumental in trotting the little girl out to get what he wanted: a couple of new laws on the books.

Four days before, while Senator Hill had been sitting in as an invited guest at the military board of inquiry in New London, he'd arranged for two bills to be introduced. One would mandate that malodorant—a distinctive, faintly repulsive scent—must be put in all natural gas as a warning agent. Another would soon be filed that would require that anyone working with gas connections be trained and certified as an engineer by the state.

Both would pass unanimously, of course. In the wake of such a mindboggling cataclysm a vote against either measure would be akin to setting the Texas flag ablaze and tossing an open Bible on top of it.

At the end of Carolyn Jones' busy day in Austin, she was proclaimed the Queen of the Senate and given some equivalent honor in the House. A bouquet of flowers was pushed into her hands and she beamed broadly while having her picture taken with legislators who lined up for the privilege. All of them had sufficient political savvy to realize the value of being seen standing compassionately beside one of the few surviving participants in the biggest news story of the time.

Two truly good laws would emerge from the New London tragedy. And good legislation was not always—some would have said never—the norm for the biennial meeting of Texas lawmakers, who engaged constantly in political turf wars and had to function within the rambling provisions and restraints of a state constitution several times longer and infinitely more confusing than its federal counterpart.

Just how much Carolyn Jones' star turns did to bring about the swift passage of those laws is questionable at best. They would have flown through without her. But the fact that she *was* there, a child who had actually lived through the horror, gave the legislators and the packed galleries in both chambers reason—even in the midst of an economic depression and with war clouds looming on the horizon—to stand up and cheer.

That one day the members of the state's legislative branch didn't bicker or bellow or, as sometimes did happen, resort to fisticuffs. For once they were in complete agreement, and were unified champions of children's safety, of goodness, and of all that is decent and pure.

And they had the photographs to prove it to the voters back home.

Forty-Four

O n Monday, March 29, just eleven days after the explosion, the London Consolidated School District resumed classes.

The school board had first considered cancelling instruction for the last two months of the spring semester, with surviving seniors completing their courses and graduating in other ceremonies in other towns. Several nearby school districts had made the offer.

But the twenty-something remaining seniors had asked to be allowed to graduate in New London, on the football field or in the gym. And Mr. Shaw, who was then still the superintendent, and most of his teachers who were still alive had thought it best to get things back to normal. Or as close to normal as possible for a school that had lost, in one fell swoop, most of its student body.

Most parents had wanted it also. And, though it might seem odd in modern times when interest in school doesn't rank as high on many students' priority list as numerous other things, the New London students *wanted* to return.

Rural schools in that era usually had excellent attendance rates. One reason was that parents, many of whom would have not had the luxury of finishing many years of formal education themselves, placed a high value on schooling. In the classic quest of the American Dream, they wanted their children to have better lives than they had, and they saw education as the most essential key to the kingdom. So, not only were the consequences of playing hooky likely stiff—and probably painful—parents instilled in their children a sense of the legitimate value of attending classes and working hard there.

Also, a reprieve from the last two months of the school year might have meant reporting for work on the family farm or, for some of the older boys, in the oil fields or the timber tracts.

But perhaps the most compelling reason for students wanting to return would have been the need to step back into the community of their peers. Or what was left of it.

In modern-day school disasters—none of which have come even close to the number of deaths or the overall horror of the New London explosion—psychiatrists, psychologists, and specially trained counselors are imported in droves to help survivors face the situation and work through it.

There is no mention of any such assistance being provided in New London.

Every student still alive when the district resumed classes had lost friends, classmates, and, in many cases, siblings. And parents grieving their lost sons and daughters were perhaps not the most comforting resources for their off-spring that were still around.

No one in that place and time would have been able to make much sense of the words *survivor* and *guilt* being put together. Common sense was held in high esteem, its value in the makeup of a truly wise person placed above just about anything else. And common sense wouldn't hold, in their opinion, with a notion that would require someone to feel guilty about something they'd had absolutely nothing to do with causing.

Still, what would become known as survivor's guilt had surely made its first inroads in those young people who had somehow lived, when so many of their classmates, friends, brothers, and sisters had died.

One of them would say, years later, that she felt like her parents were some-how disappointed in her, or mad at her. Their house was quiet and dark. And nobody talked to each other, especially about her brother, who had died in the same building that she had walked away from after the explosion. The only thing she could figure, with nobody to discuss these things, was that she must have done something wrong.

Though it would be anything but a joyful reunion, the students making their way back to the campus on the last Monday morning of March needed to go there.

The day started with an assembly in the gymnasium, behind where the junior high and high school building used to be. The windowpanes that had shattered and rained down on the PTA meeting on the eighteenth had been replaced, which was a good thing, since a freakish late season cold front had blustered its way in over the weekend, dropping temperatures significantly and leaving a dusting of snow everywhere.

Students arrived in winter coats dug out of the backs of closets or trunks, where they'd already been packed away in mothballs since most people had assumed winter was over and done with. Some still wore bandages; some had arms or legs in plaster casts. Most had scratches and scrapes. A few had no evidence of injury at all. At least on the outside.

Without being told to do so, the kids climbed up into the wooden bleachers and sat quietly with whoever showed up in their respective classes.

In addition to those who had been killed, a good many more had been moved by their parents to other schools, either placing them with relatives in other places or loading them up with the household goods, collecting the last paycheck from one oil company or another, and heading back to where they'd come from.

Some parents that withdrew their children felt guilty for having brought them there in the first place, somehow feeling it had all been their fault, and needing to make amends. Others, not a small number, were angry at Mr. Shaw, or at the school board, or at the oil industry. Some survivors would come to realize that their parents were angry—at least in part and probably not even realizing it—at other mothers and fathers whose children were still alive.

Others must have realized that seeing the place where parts of themselves had been snuffed out would just be too hard to deal with day in and day out. So they'd left, too.

Everybody shivered and nestled in their coats as the roll was called for the entire student body. Some of the names of those known to have perished were left off the list, but even then, nearly two weeks later, the roster of the dead was far from being complete. Or correct. So when each name was called out a voice might say "here." Or someone might say "she died," or simply "dead." In some cases a name was met with "moved off" or "went back to Arkansas." Or "still in the hospital."

Bill Thompson sat with the other fifth graders and half listened to the names as they were being called. Like everyone else in the big room, he pretty much knew who was dead, who was alive, who stayed put, and who moved away.

But one name caught his full attention.

"Ethel Dorsey," Mr. Duran, the high school principal, said. Ethel was the girl who had graciously traded seats with Bill a few minutes before the explosion so that he could sit behind Billie Sue Hall, who he'd felt the urge to flirt with.

"She's dead," somebody said.

Bill had somehow missed hearing about it. He looked at his shoes for a long moment, then up. He knew, even then, that every person in the building wasn't staring at him. But it felt like they were.

What he didn't know, on that cold morning, was that the long decades that lay before him would not include a single day in which he didn't think at least once of a kindhearted little girl and her last sacrifice. An unintended one, to be sure.

But, he would always realize, it was a sacrifice nonetheless.

≈

Later, when the roll call was completed and the principal and teachers had huddled together to do the necessary logistics, individual classes were sent off with teachers to various places. Some sections would meet in the gym, others in the band hall, or the homemaking building, or the art building.

There is no record of any junior high or high school classes meeting in the elementary school, which had not been damaged. Neither did any meet in churches or civic halls, as was the usual procedure when schools burned down or were badly damaged by twisters.

The sad and simple fact was there just weren't enough students left for there to be a problem finding places for them to go.

Forty-Five

O n May 6, less than two months after the disaster, the German dirigible *Hindenburg* moved, sometimes gracefully and sometimes like an awkward, discombobulated whale, depending on the fluctuating air currents, over the skyscrapers of New York.

The pinnacle of the tallest, the Empire State Building, was pointed out to the passengers assembled on the observation deck. For one of the original plans for the iconic tower that crowned the soaring edifice was that it would be a mooring for ships like the *Hindenburg*, offloading passengers down some sort of open-air contraption to a series of stairs and finally a bank of elevators. That plan was scrapped however, no doubt by someone who had visions of entire families plunging to their messy deaths in midtown Manhattan.

It was a gray, gusty afternoon, with a big storm looming over the Atlantic seaboard. So the captain of the airship had to keep her aloft until conditions improved enough to make a landing. Which meant his passengers got a few extra hours of sightseeing before floating down to the mooring tower at Lakehurst, New Jersey where it exploded, crashed, and burned.

A total of thirty-five people died in the *Hindenburg*, and one member of the ground crew. The official cause was put down as the explosion of a vast reservoir of gas.

By that time it had been finally determined that just under three hundred lives, almost all of them children, had been lost in New London's earlier encounter with the very same phenomena.

The fact that the airship's demise was caught on film as she glowed red against dark storm clouds in the late afternoon and disintegrated dramatically to the tarmac might account for that event finding a permanent niche in history and modern culture while New London was all but forgotten. That, and the fact that it was all narrated by a frantic reporter whose exclamation, "oh, the humanity!" would become part of the lexicon of not only its era but every one that came after it.

That big swastika on the rudder being chewed up by flames didn't hurt either. A strong, newsworthy symbol goes a long way when it comes to cementing images into permanence.

While the tragic afternoon in New London did garner the world's attention for a brief time, and would remain to the present day the worst school disaster in the history of the nation, there obviously just wasn't enough glamour in a country schoolhouse full of country people blowing up to let the event stay the course in people's minds.

Within a decade, and certainly within the ensuing decades, almost everyone would be completely ignorant of it.

And history, which can oftentimes be fickle, teasing at the first before the turning the cold shoulder, would move on and forget it.

This in spite of the fact that the entire bad business of March 18, 1937 left behind a subtle, yet constant, reminder.

For whenever anyone, anywhere, detects danger when about to ignite gas logs on a grate, or rekindle a pilot light on a furnace or a water heater, the faint, unpleasant odor that warns them of leaking gas is there at a cost.

Almost three hundred innocent people paid for it.

Forty-Six

The big world turned, and lost interest in New London as quickly as it had found it.

While the funerals were ongoing at an assembly line pace, reporters and photographers from across the nation packed up and went home. Walter Cronkite returned to Dallas, then back to the Kansas City bureau of United Press. Shortly thereafter he found his way to the Columbia Broadcasting System, where he would become an institution on the level of Edward R. Murrow, and where he would evolve, in due course, into everybody's Uncle Walter.

Sam Houston Allred, the baby born in the governor's mansion in Austin the night before the disaster, would have his photograph taken three days later, which would end up in the pages of the April 5 issue of *Life* magazine. In it his mother, propped up in the bed in which she'd endured the long labor and eventual birth, hands the newborn up to First Lady Eleanor Roosevelt, who grins toothily as she accepts the child, almost as if the little tableau is some sort of ritualistic sacrifice within the Democratic Party.

The baby's father, Governor Allred, was not in the picture.

This might have been a precursor of things to come.

One night that same week Pappy Lee O'Daniel, the popular radio host and flour manufacturer, recited an original poem on his show. As one of the Light Crust Doughboys scraped out a mournful elegy on his fiddle, Pappy read "A New London Mother's Midnight Prayer," which began with the following stanza:

At night when I lay on my pillow and weep
In the darkness so silent and black,
I can't go to sleep
'Cause memories creep
And it seems my dear children come back.

There were five more stanzas, each on the order of that one, and his audience ate it up, making him even more popular with the electorate that would, less than a year later, move him into the governor's mansion and into Allred's office.

Amelia Earhart ruled the headlines, airwaves, and the air itself for just four more months, before she and her navigator and her plane were all swallowed up by the Pacific Ocean.

Adolf Hitler, who'd sent the telegram to President Roosevelt lamenting the "terrible explosion which took so many young lives," would soon goosestep his way into Poland and then into many other places, finally ordering the ovens to be built that would dispatch several million people, many of them as young as the ones for whom he'd offered his "sincere sympathy."

Then there would be Pearl Harbor, and the second war to end all wars, and finally the economy would show signs of improvement about the time that Franklin Roosevelt would fall dead in the very room in Warm Springs, Georgia, where he had learned of the school explosion.

Then there would be Korea and Vietnam, making it finally clear to even the most hopeful of optimists that there really is no such thing as a war to end all wars.

And the big world turned, leaving little New London and its sad history completely hidden in its wake.

≈

Part of the reason that the 1937 explosion lost its place in the public mind, which it only really had for about a week, was that more horrific—at least in terms of body counts—disasters would follow.

The world would soon became a caldron of cataclysms, catastrophes, and calamity, courtesy of both Mother Nature and mankind.

Hitler would put to death an almost unimaginable number of people in his unique purification project—history has conveniently rounded the total off at six million—not to mention ten times that figure in the global war that raged on around it.

Typhoons, earthquakes, famines, fires, and tsunamis would devastate entire undeveloped regions of the world, racking up deaths in such high totals as to make them nearly impossible to grasp.

Terrorist strikes in virtually every civilized country on earth would keep, as Mr. Sandburg put it, piling the bodies high. Then the eleventh day of September 2001 would finally roll around, redefining forever the concept of catastrophe.

The events of that one day alone would make much that came before it pale in significance.

Especially a long ago disaster that was almost invisible already.

≈

Even the parents of the dead New London students were also partly to blame for the tragedy being lost to time.

They were proud people who kept to themselves, did for themselves, and resented intrusion, even from those wishing to assist them. They kept their distance from society in general and specifically society outside the boundaries of Rusk County. Especially after the tragedy.

Several of the oil companies offered to pay for caskets and funerals in the days following the explosion. Some parents let them; others only agreed to let the companies cosign loans at area banks. Still others refused altogether, figuring it was their responsibility, and theirs alone, to bury their dead.

That spirit of fierce independence and reliance on nobody but themselves also permeated their grief.

After the last of the funerals the Overton chapter of the American Legion, whose hall had been used as the primary morgue, collected the clothing that had been removed from bodies. They sent the items, some of them nothing more than ragged pieces of torn fabric, to a dry cleaner to be cleaned, pressed, and packaged and presented them to the parents of the dead.

The things were, as a general rule, packed quickly and carefully away in trunks or boxes with shoes, baseballs, pajamas, pocket knives, ceramic dolls, favorite storybooks, and any number of other personal effects.

Then the parents packed other things away as well.

Specifically, any mention of what happened at 3:17 on March 18.

The town closed ranks, didn't give interviews, kept completely to themselves, and all but took themselves out of the land of the living for a time.

Eventually they put pictures of their lost sons and daughters out where they could see them and got on with their lives, at least to a point. Most of them still refused to speak of the explosion or of its victims, to the press or even to each other.

Through the years several attempts were made to plan a reunion of survivors, but the parents of those who died would never hear of it. Reunions were, to their way of thinking, too close to celebrations. And nothing about that day had any reason to be celebrated.

It would be a long, long time—four decades to the day—before any official function would be held to commemorate the anniversary of the disaster.

By then, almost all of the parents would have joined their lost children in pretty graveyards, never having learned, as the survivors and friends and family finally would, that sorrow isn't something that can be buried in trunks or moved away from.

Sorrow is ambulatory, and refuses to be left behind.

Forty-Seven

On a spring afternoon in 1958 a group of boys in the senior class of New London High School were walking from their last class of the day in the main building—a handsome E-shaped replacement, put up as quickly as possible in front of where the original had stood—out to the gymnasium when they noticed an elderly man in a three-piece suit moving slowly along a sidewalk.

One of the boys, Ronny Gaudet, recognized the man as one of his great-uncles. The one, when asked about at family gatherings or church covered-dish dinners, was said to have his good days and his bad ones, the colloquial equivalent of saying he was usually sicker than well, or more muddleheaded than lucid.

Ronny stepped away from the group and walked over to touch the old fellow lightly on the arm. He asked if he could help him.

The man looked at him for a moment, then at something else.

Ronny asked if somebody was with him and, when it was obvious no one was, he asked if he'd like for him to take him home.

That's when Mr. Shaw, old and feeble, with his black tie knotted tightly at his thin neck and his fedora perched perfectly straight on his head, pointed toward a pretty patch of grass between the buildings.

"Don't you know . . ." he started. Then his bewildered look turned into one filled with purpose.

He grabbed Ronny's arm and shook it.

"There are children in there," he managed to say, in a frail voice that had lost much of its vitality, but retained enough force to deliver the next words clearly.

"My boys and girls are in there."

Part Four

Speaking Their Names

Forty-Eight

M onday is chicken and dumpling day in the London Museum and Tea Shop.

The spry old gentleman in the first booth looks doubtful when he's told the daily special. Marvin Dees never drives over to New London from Tyler on Monday but always on Wednesday, which is roast beef day. He's modified his strict routine this one time so he can meet with a pesky author and his research associate, both of whom opt for the chicken and dumplings.

Marvin motions to Jean Davidson, one of the volunteers who all serve as waiters and waitresses during the lunch rush, and asks her if the dumplings are thin or thick. When she looks confused he tells her that Floy, his wife, always rolled out mighty thin dumplings and he likes them like that.

Jean steps back to the kitchen to ask Elisa, the cook and the only paid employee in the place, about the dimensions of her dumplings and Marvin tells the author and his companion that Floy had been a fine cook.

He nods his head when he says it, and he smiles. He says they'd been married seventy years when she died.

He needed a walker to get from his car to the building when he arrived, but once settled in the booth with a glass of ice water, for it is a broiling late June day, he's a vision of health. His knitted tam, like an Irishman might wear down to the pub for a pint, sits a little forward and a tad crooked on his head, and he's tapping his thin fingers on the tabletop.

Jean comes back with the news that the dumplings aren't too thick and aren't too thin and he says he'll try them.

He'll have his ninety-fifth birthday in November. And from the looks of him it would be a safe bet that he'll make that one and some more as well.

When the plates are cleared away and the coffee cups are topped off, Marvin recounts the long afternoon and night and following morning he spent across the highway in March of 1937 when, as a young worker in the oilfields, he'd been one of the first responders to the school explosion. He tells it without hesitation and doesn't seem to mind whenever one of the two men interrupt him to ask a question or to make sure they got something down right in their notes.

He slows down a little, or stops altogether, whenever he speaks of Floy. Probably not because it's in any way painful for him, but more than likely because he wants to linger in those parts, to savor them.

He worked for the Texas Company in 1937, and stayed with them for the rest of his long career, during which time he served in every capacity from roustabout to district supervisor. He did a stint in the army during World War II, and later earned a petroleum engineering degree at Tulane while working for the company in Louisiana.

By the time he retired in 1979, at the age of sixty-three, the Texas Company had long since changed its name to Texaco and Marvin and Floy had lived all over the state, and in a few others. They bought a home in Tyler, not too far from Troup, the little town where they'd both been raised.

They were not blessed with children, though they'd wanted them. But perhaps as recompense they had been given an abundance of good years together, more than most couples, after Marvin's retirement.

In a little while Miles Toler, the director of the combination museum, archives, gift emporium, tea shop, lunch counter, café, and unofficial town meeting place, comes to refill the cups. In spite of his impressive title, Miles is just another waiter during lunch hours, and a patty flipper at the grill out back every Tuesday, which is burger day.

Marvin and Miles chat for a couple of minutes, including the two visitors in the conversation when it makes sense to, not just to be nice. Then, with no attempt at a transition Miles says two words: "pecan" and "buttermilk." Neither are questions, so the visitors don't quite know how to react.

It's a fresh dilemma for Marvin, who always comes on Wednesday, which is chocolate or apple.

Soon the author asks Marvin, over pieces of homemade pie and steaming mugs of coffee, if he can explain exactly how the people thereabouts had tapped into the pipelines for the free bleed-off gas.

He and the researcher had asked several folks the same question and, while it was obvious they *knew* how it was done, they hadn't been able to describe it sufficiently for them to understand what would appear to be a tricky and dangerous procedure.

After having his go at it, Marvin proves to be no exception.

So the researcher, much more technical minded than the author, moves in for a clarification. He begins by stating that he doesn't know much about gas or pipelines.

Marvin laughs, taps his fingers on the tabletop, and says that's pretty obvious.

Then, figuring he's explained the process sufficiently, he drinks the last of his coffee and asks the men about their families.

Forty-Nine

When Marvin Dees drives off to take care of the pair of errands he runs every Wednesday after lunch, more people come in for their midday meal, most of them such regular customers that they don't require a menu. The special will do fine, thanks.

It being summertime, the students from the high school across the street don't move in during their lunch break like a pack of hungry dogs and fill up the place. But business is good anyway, which isn't a great surprise since the only other eateries in town are a donut shop down the way and a convenience store offering prepacked sandwiches and microwaved pizza.

The volunteers on duty today dart in and out, taking orders and delivering them. Even Laverne Clifton, who is officially the archivist, comes up from her detached building full of documents, official records, newspapers, old letters, magazines, maps, and various other stacks of things to pitch in.

Laverne grew up in Conroe, north of Houston, and took her degree at the University of Texas before moving to New London to teach and coach, which she did across the highway until she retired. Then, when the museum opened she decided she'd volunteer a little, which quickly became a lot, and then became a full-time job. When Molly Ward, the first director, retired in 2005 Laverne served as the interim director until Miles Toler came on board the next year. She's as much a fixture here as the exhibits or the lunch counter.

She comes over and sits with the author and the researcher and gives them the answers to the questions they asked her earlier, about a letter one young survivor wrote to a friend in another town, and about some detail in the Bureau of Mines report. She only needed a few minutes in her treasure trove to come up with them. She hands the author a typed transcript of the letter.

He asks what his chances might be if he asked to borrow an original photograph from an exhibit to run it up to the Wal-Mart in Henderson to get a copy made.

She stretches her arm along the top of the booth's back and thinks about it. Squints.

"Well," she finally says, "I suppose you could ask." She leans forward and gives just a hint of a smile. "But you do need to understand that I'd have to kill you if you tried to take it."

She laughs. Then he laughs. Then Miles makes the copy in his office on the museum copier.

Jean Davidson's husband John brings out dishes and collects them and re-fills drinks and delivers wedges of pie after a full morning of guiding visitors through the museum. He's worked here, for no salary other than a free lunch, for a decade.

John will tell you quick enough that he's a replacement. Not in the museum and the café, but in the very fact of his existence.

His older sister, Ardyth, died across the street in the gas explosion at the age of fourteen. His parents, who never intended to have any more children, changed their mind after their daughter's death and John was born in 1940.

He and Miles, the director, were classmates in the 1958 graduating class of New London High School. That was the school's largest class in its history, partly because it was made up of so many "replacements."

Miles, a graduate of the University of Texas, moved to Tyler after retiring from the Reynolds Metals Company because he and his wife wanted to be near family. John, after graduating from Sam Houston State in Huntsville, spent his career as a cost analyst for a tire company.

Both of them were raised in New London and went to grades one through twelve across the highway. They ate no telling how many lunches in this very building—or at least part of the building—during those years, when it was the McConnico High School Drugstore. The only surviving fixture of that establishment is the lunch counter and soda fountain, which still do their jobs nicely.

Miles, who lost no siblings in the explosion, comes to work five days a week because he enjoys it, and he sees the need to keep what happened across the highway alive in people's minds.

John works every day for those reasons too. And for one more.

He wanted, when he retired, to get to know the sister he'd never met.

Ardyth's and John's parents owned and operated a grocery store and mercantile in 1937 and, unlike most couples then, had just the one child. After she was gone, they did what everybody else in town did and didn't speak of the disaster, even to each other. John was born three years after his sister's death, and never once felt unloved or uncared for. But he always knew that, even though she was seldom mentioned, part of his parents' hearts had been buried with Ardyth.

He asked his mother about her once, and since his father was not in the room, she told him about a time when Ardyth, only twelve or maybe thirteen, had wanted to learn to drive. So while her husband was at work she drove Ardyth in the family car out to a lonely stretch of country road and let her daughter bounce them both along for a bit while trying to locate the delicate balance between the gas pedal and the clutch.

John says she enjoyed telling it, even while probably feeling guilty about breaking the old, hard vow of silence that the entire town seems to have sworn to.

Jean, John's wife, says that John is more at ease since working here, and that he seems to sleep better. She graduated from New London High a year after John and Miles and is the coordinator of the tea room and café, seeing to reservations for groups and to catering jobs. Except at lunchtime of course, when she is a waitress and cashier.

This is the standard operating procedure here.

The author and the researcher begin to think they'd better finish their business and drive home before they're put to work bussing tables or washing dishes.

Fifty

The glass door that separates the tea room from the museum is actually a portal into another world.

In here, it's 1937 again.

First up is a model of the London junior high and high school, protected from curious hands by a glass case kept polished to a sparkling shine. It was meticulously built to scale, down to the exact number of panes in the windows. A wide drawer underneath can be pulled open to revel the vast crawl space where the gas collected.

The author asks Miles if they'd had it constructed because it is such a great place for visitors to begin.

Miles grins and tells him it was pretty simple. A guy offered to build it free of charge, so they thanked him.

Beyond the model, exhibit after exhibit bring that long ago era and the tragedy back to life.

Here's a radio as large as a piece of furniture, in front of which an entire family would have sat staring at the big central speaker, as if practicing for when a television set would replace it.

Here's part of a school room, with the teacher's desk up front and a chalkboard behind her chair. The student desks are old-fashioned wood and metal affairs with inkwells and carved ridges for pencils. Big Chief writing tablets and copies of My Weekly Reader lay open on scratched desktops that have been polished to a rich, dark brown by hundreds of oily palms and fingertips.

Then there is a wooden peach basket, like the many used to ferry pieces of rubble from the ruined school to the edge of the campus.

Here's a photograph of Ardyth Davidson and the rest of the softball team. That's Ardyth on the bottom row at the far right. She's smiling, looking forward to the county meet and her game. It's the last photograph ever taken of her, snapped just a couple of hours before the explosion.

Just above the photo is a remnant of Ardyth's plaid coat. The brooch is still pinned to it, its horse—or dog—broken in half, but still in midstride.

It's easy, in this room, to speculate and wonder.

Was the little boy who carried this pocketknife in his jeans killed quickly enough not to have suffered, or even to have realized what was happening? Was the little girl who wore that dress proud of the way it looked on her, or did she—like countless little girls before her and after—feel awkward enough in it to suspect that everybody was staring at her, whispering? Did the child who sat in that desk die in it? How many kids who used that enormous black telephone, as heavy as a small anvil, on Miss Patterson's desk to call home occasionally would die on that long ago afternoon? And how many would live to see great-great-grandchildren use telephones that fit in their pockets?

Another museum item is a teletype machine, like the one young Walter Cronkite leaned over to learn of the disaster. Not far away there's a button to push to hear a recorded interview when he was an old man, as he remembers his several days and nights in New London.

Here's the bulky gas regulator that was the conduit for the gas into the crawl space, giving its silent testimony as it had when laid out on a tabletop surrounded by men smoking pipes and cigarettes during the board of inquiry.

In this corner is a hospital room, everything—metal headboards of the bed, starched sheets and blanket—all brilliant white. Ominous metal forceps, scissors, and various probes and prodders lay on a stainless steel table in front of glass canisters filled with cotton balls and swabs. The walls are covered with photographs of Mother Francis Hospital, not the sprawling complex that now spills down every side of the hill, but only the white four-story original structure that had to open its doors a day early in 1937.

≈

For those who are walked through the museum by John Davidson or one of the other docents, the New London disaster pulls at different emotions in different people.

It's hardest, perhaps, for parents, since what is remembered here is, quite simply, the worst case scenario. For grandparents, it's a double hit; to imagine how difficult it would be to not only lose a grandchild, or two, or more, but to have to watch their mother or father, your own child, suffer through it.

Teachers have a hard time here. One sixth grade teacher had to step outside to compose herself because all she could think of when she saw the classroom exhibit was all those students looking at their teacher at the instant of the explosion, as if expecting her, the last person they'd see in this world, to do something to fix things. To set things right.

For other teachers, the idea of Mr. Louis Waller, who died alone in his classroom grading papers during his planning period, tugs hard. Maybe he would have turned off the overhead light and was working by the sunlight streaming in his window. Maybe he had kicked off his shoes and relaxed his feet at the end of a long day.

Maybe he died doing what he liked, what he felt called to do.

For everyone, surely, the disaster is at once a horrible waste of human life and potential and, more specifically, a very nearly unimaginable slaughter of so many children and adolescents who should, by rights, have had long lives stretching before them.

The death of children is one of the toughest conundrums to tackle. History is filled with this cruelest of ironies: the slaughter of the Holy Innocents in the first century, the doomed Children's Crusade, the much more recent collapse of the St. Mary's Orphanage in the 1900 Galveston hurricane, and, in the week before this book was sent off to the publisher, the senseless slaughter of over eighty children at a youth camp on an island in Norway.

The natural order of things requires that children should live out their time. And, while those people who have lived out a significant portion of theirs feel nothing particularly unnatural when they hear what the poet called "time's winged chariot hurrying near," they cringe when it closes in on youth. Especially when it runs down great numbers at a time.

Irony took on an even meaner tint in New London, with the explosion coming just minutes before the end of the school day, when most of the kids must have been looking out the tall windows, anticipating the outdoors on a sunny afternoon.

Some visitors are relieved when they step back into the gift shop and café. Others make it a point to return soon and see the exhibits again.

But almost all are changed.

Fifty-One

Directly behind the museum there's a medium-sized house on a street full of medium-sized houses very much like it.

Bill Thompson lives here, alone now that his wife is in a nursing home. Bill has emphysema, and has to be tethered to an oxygen hose most of the time, so it snakes along behind him as he moves slowly though the rooms.

He can't hear well, especially on the phone, so the author had to yell into the receiver to explain who he was and what he was about.

But here in his living room Bill can lean up almost to the author's face and understand him just fine.

He was in the fifth grade when the school blew up, almost immediately after he'd traded places with one girl in order to sit closer to another one. It wasn't until almost two weeks later, when the roll was being called in the cold gymnasium, that he learned that the girl who'd agreed to switch seats, Ethel Dorsey, had been killed.

He's spent most of his life struggling with the knowledge that she would have probably survived if she hadn't traded. If he hadn't asked her to.

It wouldn't be until the museum was being built in the late 1990s that he decided it was time to do something about it.

So he telephoned Ethel Dorsey's brother and asked if he'd object to him purchasing a memorial paving stone in her memory that would be set in the entryway to the museum.

When the brother told him that would be fine and thanked him, Bill took a deep breath. And a leap of faith.

"Now let me tell you why," he said.

Tears come to Bill's eyes even now when he tells about how comforting Ethel Dorsey's brother, and then her sister, were to him. He says it was like a burden was lifted when they told him he had no cause to feel a bit guilty about anything.

He breathes in more oxygen, pats the author's arm, and says it still gets to him.

Whether he's speaking of Ethel's death, her siblings' forgiveness, or the switching of those seats isn't clear.

Fifty-Two

In 1977, forty years after the disaster, a group of survivors decided it was high time they violated the unwritten vow of silence their parents had taken.

After all, many of the parents were dead by then. And those that weren't, and any survivors or siblings who protested that a celebration would be wrong would just have to be told, and hopefully convinced, that a reunion would be a celebration of life, not death.

The event was held at West Rusk High School—the school was re-named in the early sixties. There was a memorial service both in the au-ditorium and at the monument on its island in the center of the highway out front.

That March weekend in 1977 opened the floodgates. Survivors began com-municating with each other, people began answering questions about the di-saster, and the veil of secrecy, shame, and guilt was finally lifted.

When Molly Ward, who was in elementary school in 1937, organized a board of directors and began accepting financial donations in 1992 for a future museum, people started pulling things out of old crates and chests. At first it was only a trickle, a funeral announcement here, a baseball cap there. Then the stuff started pouring in, so much of it that space had to be found to store it all until it could be catalogued.

Two years later the board purchased the McConnico High School Drug-store, which had opened in 1938 while the new school was being built, and had stayed in business until 1994.

Museum volunteers set about renovating the interior. The tea room opened in 1996 and the museum in 1998. In addition to physical artifacts, doc-uments, photographs, yearbooks, and records, the archives houses transcripts of survivors' and eyewitnesses' recollections.

Eventually a pair of generous grants provided the funds necessary to ex-pand the building to double its original size, which meant that many more exhibits could be displayed on a permanent basis.

Now reunions are coordinated by the museum staff, and are held every two years. They're heavily attended.

There are fewer survivors at every gathering, of course.

For time is not only a great healer. It is a skillful harvester.

≈

The monument that stands between the museum and tea shop and the school is made of pink granite, like most of the monuments in Texas and the state capitol building as well.

It's technically a cenotaph, a monument dedicated to the dead but not housing the remains, and it rises up to an impressive forty-something feet. The apex is crowned with bas-relief sculpted images of children, hand in hand in a classical motif, with a sprinkling of ancient Egypt also, with hands and feet turned at odd angles. Some of the children are clutching schoolbooks, and they're all being comforted by a kindly, mother-like figure.

It stands on its own island in the middle of Highway 42, surrounded by a low wall made of the same pink granite, into which the names of all who died in the explosion are carved.

Almost all, anyway.

Every once in a while Miles and Laverne add a name to the list because new evidence has come their way. An old sibling or friend offers up convincing details, or an oversight just needs correcting.

Those names get added to a separate piece of granite—pink, of course, it being Texas—beside the low wall. Boyd Abercrombie's is the first name there, since his story didn't make its way home until long after the monument went up.

On the low wall itself there are several empty places among the alphabetically listed names. That's because some of the parents, back when the cenotaph was erected not long after the disaster, wanted nothing to do with it, and refused to allow their children's names to go there.

All the same, everyone knew who those children were, so room was left in case the parents came around. Some finally did, and the names were chiseled in.

Others never would be. But it didn't matter to friends and relatives, who could as easily press their fingertips against a smooth patch of granite as a chiseled one.

Remembering doesn't require much physical assistance.

≈

The cenotaph is a fine memorial, sturdy and solid and good for the ages.

But two artifacts in the nearby museum are just as fine.

One is a newspaper photograph that was published one year after the explosion, in March of 1938. In it, five smiling elementary students are seen leaning out of the open windows of a school bus. Just beneath their sun-kissed faces the words *London Independent School District* glisten on the side of the sparkling clean bus.

The caption reads:

> Smiling students of the London school happily look forward to life. They remember the tragedy which, one year ago, claimed the lives of their school and playmates, but tragedy has failed to dampen their ardor for living. Some of the students in the bus shown above most likely witnessed the explosion which took the lives of their comrades. But they continue to smile, typical of those who bore the brunt of the mishap.

In another part of the museum there are several television monitors. One is dedicated to the opening of the museum in 1998.

At that dedication, John Furr made a speech.

Sixty-one years before, he'd been the handsome, gangly blonde lad who had stood before newsreel cameras on the morning of the explosion and recited the slow, personal account that was watched by countless moviegoers across the nation.

In the section of the video that is watched by visitors to the museum, the snippet from Mr. Furr's comments, this time given as an old man, always make people nod. And sometimes reach for a tissue.

"The Greeks said," he begins, "that no one is dead, truly dead, until no one remembers them, and no one speaks their name."

He pauses, to compose himself.

"What we're doing here," he concludes, keeping a tight rein on his emotion, "is remembering."

These two exhibits might best encapsulate what the people in New London finally came to see as a very real truth.

It is possible, even in the wake of a terrible loss, to be both focused on the future, like the children on the bus, and also on the past, like the reunions and the museum.

Life, New Londoners eventually came to realize, is a constant intermingling of living and dying, of hope and sorrow. And the best way, maybe the *only* way, to get though it is to keep moving forward, even while remembering those left behind.

And remembering to speak their names.

Epilogue

Pleasant Hill cemetery is aptly named.

When the breeze whispers its way through the treetops or sends grass rolling like the surface of a pond it is indeed a pleasant hill to be on. Especially when white clouds billow up majestically into the East Texas sky, or when smaller ones drift nonchalantly along on their way to other places. It's even a nice place to be when the whole sky goes purple or gray, sending squadrons of birds scurrying ahead of a blue norther or a big thunderstorm that promises to be a gully washer.

In just one more generation the students and teachers who died in the London school will have slept there for a full century. Most of them are in a section that grew substantially over a few long-ago March days, with a nice view of thick forest and rolling farmland that is not all that different than it must have been when they were buried.

Wanda Emberling and Dale May York are there, the two girls whose bodies got mixed up for a time but finally were sorted out. And Arden Barber, the young son of Lonnie Barber, the janitor and bus driver who somehow found the resolve to deliver his full load of elementary passengers to their frantic parents before rushing back to check on his own four children.

Sammie Shoemate is there, the little girl who loved to sew and crochet and cook. And Sambo Shaw, the son of the superintendent of schools.

His father is there, too.

When Mr. Shaw finally came to his rest, no doubt a welcomed one, he was buried under pretty sky and tall trees beside his wife and son.

And among his boys and girls.

≈

Floy Dees isn't buried at Pleasant Hill, but at another graveyard not too many miles away, close to where she and Marvin grew up.

Every Wednesday, after Marvin has had his roast beef lunch and a visit with Miles and John and the rest of the volunteers, he makes two more stops before driving back to his home in Tyler.

He tells everyone that the reason for his weekly pilgrimage is the first one, to check on an oil well he still owns in the area. But everybody knows the last item on his agenda before heading home is the real motive for the trip.

When he's made his slow way over from the car, using the walker to navigate the uneven ground, he takes a few minutes to brush any branches or mown grass from Floy's grave. Usually the chore is a short one, since a week isn't much time for things to accumulate. Unless a cold front's blown in, that is, or a blustery thunderstorm, or just a good, stiff wind that gives the tall trees a thrashing, sending down limbs and leaves, pinecones and acorns.

When everything is exactly like he wants it to be, he spends a while with Floy.

A person who doesn't understand such things as a seventy-year marriage, or eternal devotion, or even stealing a few quiet moments away from the big world once a week wouldn't make much sense of these Wednesday visits.

But that wouldn't matter a bit to Marvin Dees, who has seen more life than most people, and certainly more death, almost all of it in the short span of a few hours.

What he thinks about there, be it that long life or all those deaths or something entirely different, is his own business, and he keeps it to himself. Surely he thinks of the good woman who is buried there, and of his good fortune at having lived on the earth at the same time she had, and that out of the billions of the earth's inhabitants their two little paths had managed to intersect and run together for such a good, long time.

And he must think, as the sweep and whoosh of soft wind in the tops of the tall trees chatters contentedly, of the fine reunion that lay in store for him, sometime.

Later.

Author's Notes and Acknowledgments

Having grown up in Oakwood, some eighty miles from New London, I've known about the 1937 explosion all my life.

What has always mystified me, given the nature of the disaster and the number of deaths, is that so very many people have never heard of it.

Then, when I undertook to do the research necessary to write this book I quickly learned that, though I was cognizant of the event itself, I was nearly as ignorant of the facts as all those other people.

Fifteen years before I was born my father, who was then the newly appointed superintendent of schools at Oakwood, drove to New London on the night of the explosion with several other school men from Leon County. What they did there—helping in excavation of bodies, removal of rubble, or perhaps simply standing in a large crowd held back by the National Guard—I've never known.

The reason is simple. What he saw there, or what he did there, was so horrible that he could never bring himself to talk about it. He would go on to serve in combat in the South Pacific, to deal with my mother's death, with the deaths of Oakwood students, and finally to face, toward the end of his road, the fact that he was wandering away into the shadow world of Alzheimer's. He could talk about all of those things.

But New London was off limits.

When I started my own teaching career, at about the time he was ending his, I was an English teacher and tennis coach in Palestine, another East Texas town. My team played Kilgore and Longview pretty regularly, so we drove past the New London school and its imposing monument in the middle of the highway several times a season.

Some of my high school students were totally ignorant of what happened there. Others knew a little about it.

The fact is, they probably knew about as much as I did. A case in point:

until recently I believed the school blew up because the school board or the superintendent had opted to use free, unstable natural gas.

So my compelling reasons for writing this book were to learn all I could about the event itself and its ramifications, and to tell a story that my father couldn't. And what whole generations of New London survivors and parents, friends, and siblings of victims wouldn't.

I first intended to trot out a tragic saga of greed and corruption, a sort of modern-day morality play. Then my research brought me to the official findings of the several investigations, which were all in agreement on one point: tapping into free residue gas had no bearing on the disaster whatsoever. Then I discovered Mr. Shaw, and I found a purpose I hadn't predicted.

Everyone I talked to who knew him, most of them former students, agreed he had been made something of a scapegoat when angry parents and a clambering media demanded one. Because of that, his name has been too long tainted.

For these reasons and others, the New London tragedy deserves its proper place in the history of twentieth-century America. And if this small effort proves to be in any way helpful in that regard, I will be pleased.

≈

This project would not have been possible without the kind assistance of a good many people.

First off, I am deeply indebted to Logan Kibodeaux, who served as my research associate. Our trips to East Texas were enjoyable pilgrimages, even when tromping though graveyards on broiling summer days. And I'll be eternally grateful for him driving the six hours back home each time while I looked though interview notes. Or slept.

My sister Janie and her husband Thomas Ives provided comfortable lodging for us in their hilltop vacation cabin on those trips, not to mention a couple of excellent meals.

The good people at the London Museum and Tea Shop not only opened up their vast archives and exhibits to us, but were always gracious and helpful when I'd call and ask one of my many questions, even if it was during the lunch rush.

Special thanks are owed to Miles Toler, the director, who was my most constant liaison with the museum, and to John Davidson, who allowed me to tell the story of Ardyth, the sister he never got to meet. John's wife Jean

Davidson, as well as Becky Tyner and Jerrell Herron, were particularly helpful (and patient) and archivist Laverne Clifton was kindness personified, not to mention a wealth of knowledge. All of them describe themselves as "docents, soda jerks, and waiters." I prefer to think of them as wonderfully committed to telling a little-known story. I also now am pleased to call them friends.

It was Miles Toler who thought it would be a good idea for me to meet Marvin Dees. And I'm especially grateful for that, since it was Mr. Dees who did more to fully open up the world of 1937 and the specifics of the disaster itself than any other single person.

My visit with Ronny Gaudet, the great-nephew of Mr. Shaw and a current member of the school board, helped fill in some blanks about the New London superintendent in 1937, and provided useful insight into his character.

It would be impossible to say enough about the survivors of the disaster that I interviewed, so I will let it suffice to simply say thank you, especially to Dororthy Wommack Box, Bill Thompson, and Doris Shoemate Morgan and her brother Elbert Shoemate. And Dr. Terry Hurst, DVM, was kind enough to tell me the story about his mother Sybil Jordan and her sister Mildred.

Regarding Mother Francis Hospital in Tyler, Mary Jane McNamara of the Smith County Historical Society and Jo Anne Embleton of the Roman Catholic Diocese of Tyler were most helpful. University of Texas at Tyler professor Dr. Patricia Gajda's article, "Mother Francis Hospital and the Sisters of the Holy Family of Nazareth: Fifty Years of Service," provided an abundance of useful material.

Kenneth R. Kibodeaux, PhD, a petroleum engineer and Logan's cousin, took on the formidable task of leading us through the confusing complexities of the properties and characteristics of natural gas. Architect Raymond Burroughs was helpful regarding the physical structure of the school and its crawl space. And my friend and old college roommate Jim Willett, the Director of the Texas Prison Museum, perused many a newspaper from 1937 for me. Jim and I wrote *Warden: Texas Prison Life and Death from the Inside Out* together some years ago, and I very much enjoyed working with him again.

Walter Cronkite's memoir, *A Reporter's Life,* offered valuable information regarding his several days in New London as a young journalist, and a taped phone interview of him by Molly Ward, the first director of the London Museum, provided additional details.

The wealth of archived materials at the museum is a veritable gold mine for researchers. The collection, under the watchful eye of Laverne Clifton, is impressive, including hundreds of transcripts of personal recollections, letters and journals, photographs, newspapers, magazines, school yearbooks, maps, and old almanacs. The complete published findings of the Bureau of Mines and the military boards of inquiry were particularly useful, as was an unpublished Stephen F. Austin University master's thesis in the museum collection. That meticulously researched and documented report by Mike Toon was extremely helpful regarding the exact location of individual teachers and their classes in specific classrooms at the time of the explosion.

I'm indebted to the fine staff at Texas A&M University Press, especially editor-in-chief Mary Lenn Dixon, who saw promise in the initial idea of the book and was its champion all along the road to publication. Rachel Cabaniss did stellar work as copy editor, and the book benefited greatly from her effort.

My constant proofreader Pat Soledade deserves one more round of kudos and much appreciation, as does my literary agent Jacques de Spoelberch. Pat, Jacques, and I have trekked through many a project now and weathered many a storm. The journey has always been better for them having been along.

Finally, one more expression of appreciation to my wife Karen, who has put up with my research junkets, countless hours of my being sequestered in my study at the keyboard, and my occasional bouts of moodiness without ever complaining.

To all, many thanks. Any mistakes in the narrative are completely mine, and not theirs.

Ron Rozelle
November, 2010

Their Names

This list of those who died in the explosion of the London Consolidated School on March 18, 1937, or later from injuries received there, was compiled by the staff of the London Museum, who acknowledge possible omissions and errors in spelling owing to lost records. The list is revised whenever new information is provided.

Boyd Abercrombie
Evelyn Bonnie Adams
Almita Fae Allmon
Allene Myrtle Anderson
Lillian Laverne Anderson
Betty Ruth Apple
Ruth Louise Arnold (teacher)
Wayne Scott Arnold
Arden Leon Barber
Ollie B. Barber
Nellie Barnes (teacher)
Donald Barrett
Edward T. Barrett Jr.
Pauline Barrett
Lavern Tilden Barton
Murvin Harland Barton
Margaret Louise Baucum
Laura Elizabeth Bell (teacher)
Mary Frances Bennett
Betty Lou Benson
Nellene Bishop
John A. Blackerby Jr.
Elvin Neale Blackford

Virginia Rose Blanton
George Atmon Bonner
Oneita Bonner
Henry Bryan Bowlin
Sybil Dell Braden
Eloise Elizabeth Brister
Bobbie Lorine Brown
Elaine W. Brown
Naoma Bunting
Lemmie R. Butler (teacher)
John Robert Buzbee
Owen Byron
Mary Prisilla Carney
Chloe Ann Carr
William Polk (Billy) Childress
Murray Dixon Cloate
Mildrid Louise Clair
Mary Lynn Clark
Byron D. Clover
Forrest E. Coker
Helen Cole
Charles Rusk Collins Jr.
Kenneth D. Corrie

Perry Lee Cox
Annie Belle Crim
Jimmie Wilmot Crumbley
Marcella Cummings
Betty Lou Curlee
Zana Jo Curry
Jacqueline Cuvelier
Jane Damuth
Annie Laurie Davidson
Ardyth Davidson
Helen Adams Davidson
Joseph Wheeler Davidson Jr.
June Davis
Kenneth Wayne Davis
Dorothy Ann Dearing
Travis Hardy Dial
Wanda Joyce Dickenson
Alice Dorsey
Ethel Dorsey
Winnifred Melvene Drake
James Alfred Duncan
Vera Virginia (Sue) Duncan
Forrest Eugene Eakes
Holly Jo Ellison
Edwin Zone Elrod
Juanita Elrod
George Lee Emberling
Wanda Louise Emberling
Doris Nell Etheredge
James Patrick Fealy
Jack Fentress
John Arnold Ford
Mary Elizabeth Ford
Mary Ellen Forman
Emaloyd Francis
Marjine Francis
Myrtle Marie Freeman

Carl Hamilton Frey Jr.
Martha Jean Gandy
Eddie Herman Gauthreaux (visitor)
Allen T. Gerdes
Alvin H. Gerdes
G. W. Gipson
Marcelyn Carol Gipson
R. A. Goff Jr.
Betty Kathryn Gordon
Joe Curry Gordon (post graduate)
Mrs. John W. (Emma) Gore
    (teacher)
Paul Greer
Edwin Grigg
Tom Howard Guinn
Harun David Gunn
Norris Thurston Hale
Emma Irene Hall
Oscar Grady Hall Jr.
Carl Hammilton Jr.
Francis Hankins
Masel Lorene Hanna (teacher)
Laneta Fay Hardie
Alita Fay Hardy
G. J. Hardy
Martha Jane Hargis
Coy Dee Harrelson Jr.
Helen Louise Harrelson
Betty Joe Herrington
Mary Ellen Herrington
James W. Harris
Charles Edward Hasbrook Jr.
Yvonne Jackolene Hathaway
Graham Keith Henson
Juanita Herron
Betty Jo Hodges
Irma Elizabeth Hodges

Earnestine Hogue

Margretta Hogue

Bessie Estelle Holland

Betty Kathryn Holleyman

Jessie Elinor Holt

Mary Frances Hooten

Imogene Houser

Laura Lee Houser

Martha Ellen Houser

Elijah Hudson

Elisha M. Hudson

Hubert H. Hudson

Melba Lee Hughes

Charles Porter Hunt

Lena J. Hunt (teacher)

Ruby Francis Hunt

Maxine Jacobs

Kenneth Johnson

Geneva Lucille Jolly

Charles Goodall Jones

Fedelia Lee Jones

Helen Charlotte Jones

Maudine Kelly

William Artice Ketchum

Claudell Kilgore

Mary Lois King

Ernest Ray Knipe

Rachel Mae Knotts

Robert Lee Krauss

Martin Krause

Robert Austin Lambert

Homer Clint Latham

W. D. Latham Jr.

Anna Mae Lechtenberg

Helen Lechtenberg

Florence Ruby Lee

Mary Ellen Lehew

Arzell Lloyd

Mary Emily Lloyd

Virginia Allene Loe

Helen Charlotte Lowe

John A. Lumpkin Jr.

Donald Robert McChesney

Vincent Harold McClure

Lanny McCune

Jack McGovney

James McGoveny

W. C. McLawchlin

Shirley Lataine McQuaid

J. E. Maddry

Ida Maxine Maddry

Doris Manck

Louise E. Martin

Blondell F. Maxwell

Charles Henry Maxwell

Louise Maxwell

Evelyn Jo Mayhew

William Floyd Meador Jr.

Doris Ray Melton

Arliss Ray Middleton

Carroll Evaughn Miller

Sebe C. Miller Jr.

Sarah Jane Mills

Annie Marie Milstead

Alma Louise Monday

Mrs. Clarence (Billy) Moore (visitor)

Dessie Lometa Moore

Billie Jake Morefield

Marion Wayne Mote

Patty Anna Mote

Marjorie Louise Myers

Shirley Elizabeth Myers

John Worthley (Jack) Nail

Mary Ethel Neal (teacher)
Johnnie Marie Nelson (teacher)
Aubrey Lee Netherton
Orrin Neal Newell
Jackie Mae Newnham
Betty Mozelle Norton
Vester Allen Norton
Charles Harrell O'Neal
Raymond B. O'Neal
Marie Patterson (Mr. Shaw's secre-
    tary)
Joyce Jenell Payne
Lewis Mallernee Payne
Edna Ruby Peace
Forest Lavon Person
James Ray Petty
James Henry Phillips (visitor)
Roseann Phillips
Twillia Ruth Phillips
Virgil B. Phillips
Hazel Marie Pierson
Ola Christine Platt
Edna Elizabeth Powell
Mattie Queenie Price (teacher)
Lloyd Garland Pride
Lonnie Pride
John Henry Propes (teacher)
Anna Ray Purcell
Gabe A. Ragsdale Jr.
Aubra B. Rainwater
Evelyn B. Rainwater
Helen Jo Rainwater
Delores Ray
Curtis Barton Reams
Ruby Earline Reed
James Basel Rhodes
Dorothy Mae Richardson

Betty Jane Rider
Charles Oliver Rider
Billy Roberts
Holton Dean Roberts
Norma Wayne Roberts
R. B. Roberts
Willie Ruth Roberts
Anna Maxine Rogers
Thomas Blanton Rogers
Louise Rowell
Esther Faye Rucker
Robert Henry Sallee
Robert Basil Salyer
David Willard Scott
Earl Jefferson Scott
Inda Maudine Sevens
Clifton (Sambo) Shaw
Dorothy Oleta Shaw
Marvin Shaw
Robert Wayne Shoemaker
Sammie Lee Shoemate
Abner Lavelle Smith
Bobbie Jean Smith
Iva Jo Smith
Mattie Mae Smith
Sam Ross Smith Jr.
Willien Ruth Smith
Anna Maude Smoot
Helen Smoot
William Edward Sowell
Carl Francis Staggs
Marshall Starks
Geraldine Stearns
Henry Lee Steele
Philo Stephens
Maudine Stephens
Howard Lee Stone (post graduate)

W. Stubblefield
Glendell Sutherlin
Lawrence Albert Swift
Willie H. Tate (teacher)
James Pickney Tatum Jr.
Charles Ray Taylor
Marjorie Evelyn Thiebaud
Lizzie Ella Thompson (teacher)
Mildred Louise Thompson
Walter Thompson
Billy Tipp
Rose G. Van Haverbeke
Mary Elizabeth Vines
Anna Belle Waggoner
Euda Alice Walker (visitor)
Herman Lawrence Walker
Mary Inez Walker
Annie Morine Walker

Louis Waller (teacher)
Florine Warren
S. Jack Warthan
Ammie Lois Watkins
Katie Mae Watson (teacher)
Mary Jo Webb
Doris Lucille Wells
Dorothy Joyce White
Aubry Williams
Doris Dean Williams
Erma Gene Williams
Mary Lou Willis
Bernice Cleo Womack
Glenn Turner Wood
Thomas Malcolm Wooley
Doris Wyche
Dale May York
Mozelle York

Subject Index